Serious Money

How to make and enjoy it

Barrie Pearson

Published in 2005, reprinted 2006

Thorogood Publishing Ltd
10-12 Rivington Street
London EC2A 3DU
Telephone: 020 7749 4748
Fax: 020 7729 6110
Email: info@thorogoodpublishing.co.uk
Web: www.thorogoodpublishing.co.uk

A CIP catalogue record for this book is
available from the British Library.

PB: ISBN 1 85418 310 9

Cover and book designed and typeset in
the UK by Driftdesign

Printed in India by Replika Press

With huge thanks to my family, friends, work colleagues,
business acquaintances, and countless other people
who inspired and helped me to become richer and truly happy.

The Author

Barrie Pearson was not born with a silver spoon but with cerebral palsy and hemiplegia, acute paralysis of his left arm and leg. At the age of six, he was offered a place for life in a residential home for the seriously mentally or physically disabled. His parents were a labourer and a domestic cleaner.

But by the age of six he could write and read much better than his parents, and had a demonstrable flair for making money. He already had the overwhelming belief that his disability was an unfair advantage which would help him to become seriously wealthy and truly happy.

The rest of his life to date is truly inspirational. He graduated in Theoretical Chemistry, became a qualified accountant, and enjoyed outstanding success as an executive in multinational companies. In 1976, he founded *Livingstone Guarantee*, the first corporate finance boutique in the UK which became the largest and most successful in the industry, before he sold it for a substantial sum in 2001. Then he formed *Realization*, to provide world class mentoring and coaching to help entrepreneurs to groom their company for sale and to realize their wealth.

In his spare time, he has been a worldwide seminar presenter, written a dozen books, and has spent 20 years as a leading restaurant critic – even though he is unable to use a knife and fork.

More importantly, along the way he has helped many people to become seriously richer and truly happy. He knows he was born lucky. This book has been written to inspire you and to show you how you can become seriously wealthy and truly happy. He passionately wants some of his inspiration and good luck to rub off on you.

Contents

Introduction

At any age from your teens to a senior citizen, this book has the power to guide, to motivate and to inspire you to become seriously richer and happier, regardless of whether you are in dire financial straights or already wealthy. It has been written to channel your imagination and to galvanize you into action so that inevitably you will be seriously richer and happier.

The book is gimmick free, because there are no workable gimmicks for wealth and happiness, instead it is crammed full of simple, practical and proven techniques which have worked in abundance for me and countless other people I have helped. You probably feel you really would like to believe this book will make your seriously richer and happier, which you really long for, but remain sceptical.

You have to admit, however, that being born with cerebral palsy and hemiplegia, severe paralysis of my left hand, arm and leg, to parents who were a labourer and a cleaner did not promise wealth and happiness for me. Importantly, my parents were very happy. Even more importantly, there was absolutely no reason why I could not become seriously rich and happy. At six years old, I was offered a place for life in a residential home for severely physically and mentally disabled people. What nonsense! By then I could walk, attended school, could read and write well, but already had the knack of making money as well.

In our village, it was a tradition that children visited houses on Christmas morning to sing a carol and receive money. My singing voice has always been awful but it did not deter me, and there was an even more lucrative tradition that the first carol singer at each house received more money than those who followed later. I got up really early and only sang for the eight largest houses. My pals would open their presents first and sing at every house until they lost their voice, but earned less than me. I quickly learned not to brag about success and never shared my secret with them.

A golden key is

Always identify and pursue the jugular vein of opportunity in any situation.

My father had a large garden and was so passionate about his beloved daffodils, tulips, roses and dahlias that he would not let my mother cut any flowers for the house because it would spoil his display and might weaken the plants. At seven years old I had a great idea, namely to sell the flowers. He was appalled, I persisted and persisted, but he eventually relented and accepted my offer of 25% of all sales for himself.

Every Saturday and Sunday morning, I sold the flowers door to door in our village, carrying them in an old zinc bucket filled with water to demonstrate their just cut freshness. My 13 year old sister refused to help me because she felt it was too embarrassing. Fortunately, we lived on a busy main road, so I put up a sign and displayed the flowers. My sister was quite happy to serve the customers and take their money.

Another golden key is

When you have a sure fire idea to make money don't just persist, make Robert the Bruce look like a premature quitter if necessary.

By the age of 36, I had enjoyed a successful executive career in multinational companies. So much so, that a top headhunter told me I was so highly paid that I had become virtually unemployable by another company. This was in the 1970s, when the approach to executive pay was much more age related and conservative than today. Then someone said to me 'if you start a corporate finance advisory firm, my company will be your first client'. I had the requisite skills and experience from my executive career, but had never been a professional adviser.

I made an instant decision to go ahead, which was rash despite the successful outcome because I did no research whatsoever. I bought a cheap desk, located it in our dining room, and persuaded my wife to learn to type and become my secretary. If it did not succeed, I was confident I could resume my executive career, not necessarily at the previous level, but older and wiser. I told four firms of headhunters that I was taking a calculated risk and asked for their help to get another job if the need should arise, and all readily agreed. Fortunately, *Livingstone Guarantee* had become the largest independent corporate finance house in the UK when I sold it in 2001.

Another golden key is

Always assess the downside risk and have a deliverable contingency plan in case of failure, even if the possibility is remote.

Many years ago a stunningly beautiful young woman worked in my team in a routine clerical role, which she really hated. She asked for my advice because she said she had neither qualifications nor skills, and was doomed to suffer boring jobs. She admitted to a dream of working in a glamorous industry such as 'fashion'. Other women in the office recognized she had a real skill with make-up and would ask her advice. I persuaded her to take a specialist course in make-up and to set her sights on a job in television. She quickly became a senior make-up artist and then her talent landed her a lucrative make-up job and international travel in the world of major feature films.

Another golden key is

Recognize your latent ability and be
prepared to seek advice and act upon it
if it makes sense.

A friend of mine started an information technology support services business and it grew steadily and profitably for 10 years. Then he decided to go for rapid growth and hire several expensive staff, the expected sales growth never happened, a major contract was not renewed and there was a sharp downturn in the sector. The business plunged into loss and the bank was pressing for a hefty personal guarantee to support the increased borrowing. He said "I'm going to let the business fold, walk away and start again in a different business". The situation was curable and I persuaded him to chop the overheads drastically in order for the business to survive and to save as many jobs as possible. Within six months, the business was back in profit and has progressed further since then to achieve a record annual profit.

Another golden key is

When you face major problems, stiffen your resolve, don't procrastinate and be prepared to take calculated and drastic action as necessary.

There are many, many more real life success stories I could tell you, but we need to concentrate on helping you to become seriously richer and happier, without delay.

It is important at the outset that you understand the available routes to becoming seriously richer and happier. When you begin to think about it you will profit from the secrets in this book because they are so simple and obvious.

The legal ways of becoming seriously richer are really quite mundane, namely:

1 saving
2 investment
3 achieving more career success
4 becoming self-employed or starting a business

5   a management buy-out or buy-in by senior executives

6   finding a rich spouse or partner

but definitely not by pure gambling!

The real secret is to become seriously richer, and happier as well. Some people do become seriously richer, and seriously unhappy. The price of wealth could be mental breakdown, stress, divorce, alcoholism, drugs and so on.

The first part of the book will guide you to achieve the wealth and success you want. The second part deals with creating a really happy and healthy life and retirement. It is a huge mistake to sacrifice everything for wealth first and only then to seek serious happiness, because it may be too late to achieve the particular happiness you always wanted or have already lost.

The ultimate golden key is

Always pursue a wealth and happiness balance in your life.

Now begin to turn your idle dreams into tangible achievement by reading and actioning the rest of this book.

Part One

Achieve the wealth and success you dream about

WHEN TRAVELLING BY ROAD, YOU NEED TO KNOW WHERE YOU ARE STARTING FROM IN ORDER TO PLAN A ROUTE TO YOUR DESIRED DESTINATION

Take stock, and set your financial goals

YOUR SITUATION MAY BE BETTER than you think, or much worse. You may have pressing financial problems and be unable to see any way forward. You probably have idle dreams, but feel they will remain impossible dreams. Whatever your situation, this chapter sets out the positive action you need to take:

1   stock of your present financial situation

2   prioritize your financial problems and address them effectively

3   review and reorganize your financial assets and liabilities

4   think about the annual income and capital wealth needed to make you much happier

5   decide the commitment and sacrifice you are ready to make

6   set your income and capital goals

7   create your personal 10 year vision for becoming seriously richer and happier

8   commit to a month by month action plan

Each of these steps will be considered separately.

Take stock of your financial situation

When travelling by road, you need to know where you are starting from in order to plan a route to your desired destination and the same is true with your personal finances. Boring though it may sound, it is essential that you record your income and expenditure. You need to know whether you are slowly but surely sinking deeper into debt, about making ends meet, or you have surplus income which should be invested. Your outgoings need to be separated into essential or discretionary, because it may be that indulgences and impulse spending are either pushing you into debt or denying you the opportunity to start accumulating wealth. To get an accurate picture, quarterly, half-yearly and annual items must be taken into account. The following table will help you to assess your income and expenditure.

The simple steps involved are:

A   record your income line by line in the appropriate column

B   sub-total each column

C   multiply each sub-total by the figure shown to calculate the annual figure

D   enter the annual figures in each column

E   add up all the figures in D to calculate your annual income.

Estimated income and expenditure statement

INCOME

A	Weekly	Monthly	Quarterly	Half-yearly	Annual	
State Income						
Savings						
Salary						
Overtime						
Bonus						
Profit Share						
Interest						
Dividends						
Pension						
B Sub-Total						
C Multiply by	X 52	X 12	X 4	X 2		
D Annual Total						E

Essential expenditure

A	Weekly	Monthly	Quarterly	Half-yearly	Annual	
Mortgage payments/rent						
Loan repayments						
Property and local authority taxes						
Heating and lighting						
Water charges						
Property maintenance						
Food						
Clothes						
Travel						
Telephone						
Other						
B Sub-total						
C Multiply by	x52	x12	x4	x2		
D Annual total						E

Discretionary expenditure

A	Weekly	Monthly	Quarterly	Half-yearly	Annual	
Car purchase payments						
Vehicle or road tax						
Car insurance						
Car repairs						
Hire purchase payments						
Eating out						
Leisure						
Gifts						
Holidays						
Other						
B Sub-total						
C Multiply by	x52	x12	x4	x2		
D Annual total						E

You may feel that some of the items classified as discretionary are essential, but the point is that these can be reduced or eliminated if necessary, although perhaps not immediately.

Now produce your income and expenditure summary using the following table:

Annual income and expenditure summary

INCOME
less Essential expenditure _____

SUB-TOTAL
less Discretionary expenditure _____

Annual surplus/(deficit) _____

If your essential expenditure exceeds your income, doing nothing means that your situation will get worse. Visit your local Citizens Advice Bureau or community support group to find out if you are receiving the maximum possible state help. Seek some part-time work which will fit into your lifestyle, even if it is only a few hours a week. This will improve your finances and, more importantly, enhance your self esteem and determination to overcome your problems. I am not suggesting that it is easy, and the first steps will be difficult, but please do make a start.

Another possibility is that your income exceeds your essential expenditure, but you overspend on discretionary items, impulse purchases and indulgences. You know that if you really want to be richer and happier, you must trim back your spending and ideally plan to have a surplus which you can invest regularly.

Prioritize and address your financial problems

It may be that your financial difficulties are temporary, perhaps because of redundancy or ill-health, if so, there is action you can take, such as:

- ask your mortgage provider for a 'repayment holiday' until you are earning again, rather than risk your home being repossessed

- persuade the local authority or your landlord to allow you some deferral of rent

- explain your situation to your bank manager and seek an overdraft or an increased facility temporarily.

The key is to enlist help from the people you owe money to before they take punitive action against you.

Review and reorganize your financial assets and liabilities

Debt causes stress and worry, which may materially contribute to ill-health and make matters worse. Exorbitant interest rates can compound the situation. Some store credit cards charge an interest rate of 30% or more. Credit cards offering an interest free transfer of your balance from another card, may charge a high interest rate on all new purchases. Unauthorized overdrafts are a handsome source of profit for banks by charging an 'arrangement fee' and a high rate of interest.

So the first step is to assess your assets and liabilities by writing them down on the following table, or by producing your own computer spreadsheet.

Personal assets and liabilities

ASSETS

    Market value of home

    Less mortgage

    Equity in home

    Current bank account

    Deposit accounts

    Tax free saving schemes

    Stock market investments

A TOTAL ASSETS

LIABILITIES

    Loans .

    Hire purchase debts

    Overdraft

    Credit cards

    Other

B TOTAL LIABILITIES

C NET ASSETS/LIABILITIES

C Your net assets/liabilities is calculated by A minus B

THE KEY IS TO ENLIST HELP FROM THE PEOPLE YOU OWE MONEY TO BEFORE THEY TAKE PUNITIVE ACTION AGAINST YOU

Your aim should be to:

- minimize your borrowing costs
- improve the return on your savings

The cheapest form of borrowing is a mortgage on your home, so consider taking the opportunity to increase your mortgage and obtain a better rate of interest so that you can repay expensive borrowing such as credit cards, hire purchase agreements and overdraft. Another option worth considering is a combined mortgage and current account, which could deliver worthwhile interest savings by using any credit balance on your current account. The trap which must be avoided, however, is to repay your various debts by taking out a larger mortgage and then begin accumulating more credit card, hire purchase and overdraft debts.

Current account balances often pay a miserable 0.1% interest at best, which is why a combined mortgage and current account saves you money by reducing your mortgage balance by sacrificing your 0.1% interest income. Some banks pay a poor savings rate. So, alternatively, check out 'best buy' savings rates in newspapers and websites to find a worthwhile rate of interest, and review your savings every few months to ensure you are still receiving a competitive rate of interest.

Consider the income and wealth you want to be much happier

Now that you know what your annual income and expenditure are, together with your assets and liabilities, you need to think about the income and wealth which will make you much happier. Many people imagine, quite wrongly, if you win one million in the lotto tomorrow then you will be able to retire immediately and live a life of luxury.

Interest rates are currently low, and likely to remain so for quite a while yet. For a top rate tax payer, the net income from savings is likely to be about 2% a year. Stock market returns may average only about 4% a year during the next few years. So a realistic net of tax income is only about 3% from a mix of savings and safer stock market investments. So to become an instant millionaire, and retire immediately, will give you an income of about 30,000 a year, which cannot be described as providing you with a millionaire lifestyle. Furthermore, inflation will gradually erode your purchasing power as the years pass.

I believe your starting point should be to consider your current income and expenditure and decide what level of income is needed for you to enjoy a wealthier and happier lifestyle. If you find it helpful, rework your expenditure statement to reflect what you would like to enjoy and then decide the annual salary, before the deduction of income and other taxes, to provide it.

REVIEW YOUR SAVINGS EVERY FEW MONTHS

Unless you earn a huge income, saving from your income alone is unlikely to enable you to accumulate serious capital wealth. The most likely avenues are starting your own business, developing property or marrying a rich partner.

Decide your commitment and sacrifice

You need to decide the commitment and sacrifice you are prepared to make, and for how long. For example, if you need to accumulate £15,000 in order to have the deposit to buy your first home, are you prepared to:

- Give up foreign holidays for, say, two years?
- Do an additional part-time job?
- Stop smoking?
- Spend time and money to gain a qualification to increase your earning power?
- Ask a relative for a loan and demonstrate that you can repay a mortgage and a monthly repayment on their loan?

You need to remember, however, the importance of balancing time spent getting richer and enjoying a happier life. If you become a workaholic your health and your family are likely to suffer. So it is important to set a realistic period for the single minded pursuit of wealth or you are likely to discover and suffer the consequences later.

Set your income and capital goals

This is not about idle dreams. It is about making a personal commitment to yourself; to achieve goals you set for yourself. So be realistic!

I suggest you set yourself annual income goals for the next 12 months, 3 and 5 years ahead. By far the most important of these is the next 12 months. When you achieve your goal for the first 12 months, your confidence in your ability to achieve your goals will soar. So I repeat, be realistic. You can and should always review your goals annually, and where appropriate set your sights higher.

IT IS ABOUT MAKING A PERSONAL COMMITMENT TO YOURSELF; TO ACHIEVE GOALS YOU SET FOR YOURSELF

To test your goals at the outset, you should write down the evidence and reasons why you believe they are achievable. If you are not convinced, it is unlikely they will happen and you should lower them.

Capital goals are difficult to set meaningfully, and they might just be pie in the sky. I remember about 10 years ago, a 28 year old said to me "I am going to be a millionaire within 10 years, I just know it". His approach was breathtakingly simple and equally naïve. "I have £8,000 of cash and I will invest it so that it doubles every year. Within 7 years I will be a millionaire". There was no plan. He is no richer today, works at a fitness club and blames repeated bad luck.

Another acquaintance of mine is nearly 50, and for the last 15 years has been hell bent on becoming a billionaire. He has backed a string of individuals to pursue revolutionary products and business propositions, but each one has failed sooner or later. He is no wealthier at all today, but his relentless quest continues. In sharp contrast, if he had started a business 15 years ago and worked hard to grow it, I feel sure he would be at least a multi-millionaire today.

It makes sense to set 1, 3 and 5 year goals for capital accumulation as well. As with income goals, but even more importantly, you need to write down the evidence as to why your one year goal is achievable. For example, you have decided to trim your personal outgoings to that you will commit to invest £100 each month in a unit or mutual trust fund. After a year you will have invested £1,200 and hopefully your holding with be worth, say, between £1,250 and £1,500, but probably not more.

An alternative plan could be to sell your present home because it does not have development potential and buy a property where you can add real value by, say, remodelling the kitchen and building an extension. Your plan may be to sell the property within a year and to start again on a bigger property. Some people have done this several times and now own a mortgage-free house worth a million or more. You need to do a lot of homework, research and careful financial projections before you can meaningfully set your capital goal for even a year ahead. Also, it must be remembered that success is easier in a rising property market, but a falling one could rule out realizing any capital gain for some years.

Create your personal 10 year vision for wealth and happiness

The purpose of this is to write down on a single sheet of paper a description of the lifestyle you want to enjoy in 10 years time. Why? So that you can remind yourself every single day what you are trying to achieve. Not only will this help to focus your conscious efforts to achieve it but, more importantly, the power of your sub-conscious will help without you really being aware of what is happening.

One thing is worth repeating again, however, the importance of becoming wealthier and happier. There is a point for everyone where the excessive pursuit of wealth undermines or even ruins happiness.

Happiness does not necessarily follow increased wealth, so don't set your sights too high.

Your personal vision statement is entirely subjective, and will be quite different for a 25 year old compared to someone of 55. An illustrative 10 year personal vision statement for a 30 year old single woman follows:

Illustrative 10 year personal vision statement

Home	I will live in a detached house in a village, having moved out of the city.
Career	My interior design skills will have been used to create my own business.
Family	I will have children and be able to afford to send them to boarding school in due course.
Wealth	I will have tangible assets, separate from my home and business, worth at least £100,000.

REMIND YOURSELF EVERY SINGLE DAY WHAT YOU ARE TRYING TO ACHIEVE

I am not suggesting that your home, career, family and wealth should be part of your personal vision. It should be what you really want, so other things which might feature include:

Travel	I will have saved enough money to have spent a year travelling in Asia.
Charity	I will have spent a year working on an aid project in Africa.
Redirection	I will have completed a full-time course in photography and earn my living as a commercial photographer.
Escape	I will have left the city and the rat race behind to live a simple life in a remote spot.

Very few people are able to sit down and write their 10 year personal vision statement immediately. You may need days, weeks or months to formulate your vision. My message to you, however, is to start work on it now and recognize the importance of having a written statement.

Commit to a month by month action plan

By now, hopefully you will have taken stock of your financial vision, set some goals and created your 10 year personal vision statement. Unless you commit yourself to taking positive action, however, increased wealth and happiness may prove disappointingly slow to materialize or even elusive. So complete the following personal action plan.

Personal monthly action plan

MONTH	ACTION TO BE TAKEN	RESULTS TO BE ACHIEVED
1		
2		
3		
4		
5		
6		
7		

MONTH	ACTION TO BE TAKEN	RESULTS TO BE ACHIEVED
8		
9		
10		
11		
12		

A typical entry may be:

MONTH	ACTION TO BE TAKEN	RESULTS TO BE ACHIEVED
MARCH	Cut up my store cards and begin to pay off the balances	
APRIL	Research combined mortgage and current account productions	
MAY		Store credit card balances paid off
JUNE		Different mortgage arranged at a lower interest cost

Key point summary

1   establish your current annual expenditure, so you can compare your income and outgoings

2   identify and tackle any pressing financial problems

3   establish your capital worth, or debts, and reorganize your assets and liabilities

4   set income and wealth goals you truly believe you can achieve

5   create your own 10 year personal vision for wealth and happiness

6   set your own month-by-month action progress and monitor your achievement

2 Vital touchstones to create serious wealth

SOME PEOPLE THINK THAT YOU are either born with a knack for making money, or not. Nonsense! It is true that some people seem to have a highly developed instinct from an early age, but everyone can develop these traits. The vital touchstones for creating serious wealth include:

1 get to really know yourself
2 turn you dreams into conviction, belief and reality
3 identify and lock onto the jugular vein of opportunity
4 rehearse success daily
5 develop your self-esteem
6 good luck is an attitude of mind
7 exploit your talents
8 regard disability as an unfair advantage
9 assess the upside and downside of risks... always

10 respect people and beware of arrogance

11 pursue a personal action plan

Each of these will be considered separately.

Get to really know yourself

It is important to really know yourself, yet some people go though life either not doing so or perhaps simply denying the reality to themselves.

Questions you need to answer about yourself include:

- **What is holding you back from being wealthier?**
- **What is letting you down?**
- **What mistakes do you repeat?**

The key is to define the problems because this is a major step to find deliverable solutions. For example, you may be a single father with young children who need to be taken to and from school, and looked after during school holidays. As a result, you may not have felt able to work for some time but you can find part-time work to suit your schedule and possibly team up with another single parent to share childminding.

Quite often, we don't see ourselves as other people see us. Subconsciously or consciously you may feel a victim of repeated bad luck. To get to know yourself better, ask your parents, siblings and close friends to be candid with you.

Turn your dreams into conviction, belief and reality

You may be thinking 'if only'. Well, it happens for many other people, so why not for you? It simply requires a positive mental attitude, properly channelled, to make it happen for you.

You have already made a start, perhaps without realizing it. Your 10 year personal wealth vision statement you prepared in Chapter 1 is the vital first step. Conviction needs to come next, by writing down the evidence and the reasons why it will happen. Then it is a short step to turn conviction into belief. You need a personal commitment to take action and the staying power not just for months but for years, to make it happen.

Identify and lock onto the jugular vein of opportunity

I use this phrase unashamedly to urge people always to be looking for the really big opportunity which is relevant and right for you. Many people set their sights on a logical improvement, or worse still wait for it to happen to them, rather than identifying a major opportunity.

For example, at work people tend to look for an opportunity to be promoted to the next grade. Smarter people will be continually looking for an unexpected and major opportunity, such as volunteering to join a new division or an overseas start-up within the group, because it is expected to grow rapidly, and will provide the prospect of fast-track promotion.

IT IS A SHORT STEP TO TURN CONVICTION INTO BELIEF

You may be employed in a sales support role, with a modest salary, whilst sales executives earn much more and can progress to senior management roles. Worse still, it may be unprecedented for someone to transfer from a support role to sales executive in the company. If this is the jugular vein of opportunity for you, however, then you must cajole and persuade to create the opportunity for yourself.

Perhaps you are a lowly paid, but experienced gardener working in a public parks department, but you have a flair for garden design. The jugular vein of opportunity for you may be to start a part-time business of your own, working during weekends, until you are confident there is a full-time demand for your services.

Many people, perhaps you as well, have the jugular vein of opportunity within your reach right now and fail to either recognize it or pursue it. You need to ask yourself – what major opportunity is staring you in the face?

Rehearse success daily

Channel your conscious mind, and your sub-conscious will follow suit, to focus everyday on your 10 year personal wealth vision statement. Literally read it every single day.

Rehearse in more tangible ways as well. I believe it was no accident that Harold Wilson, a post-war UK Prime Minister, was photographed standing on the step of 10 Downing Street as a young boy. Whether it was conscious or not, he was rehearsing his success in a most powerful way.

ASK YOURSELF

WHAT MAJOR OPPORTUNITY IS STARING YOU IN THE FACE?

If you work in sales support and want to become a highly paid sales executive, you can rehearse success as follows:

- get to know some of the sales executives
- ask them, and your boss, if you can accompany them on sales visits occasionally, where you can play a credible sales support role
- ask the sales executives how they managed to get into a sales career and what advice they recommend to you
- tell your boss, in a suitable way, that you are keen to pursue a sales career but want it to be within the company

You may quibble with my use of the words 'rehearsing success' but it is all about getting the feel of and experiencing a taste of the success you want.

Develop your self-esteem

Self-esteem seems such an elusive quality to some people, almost to the point of questioning the existence of it, yet it is so vital for success. Put very bluntly, the winners in life tend to have high self-esteem, whilst the losers have low self-esteem.

Put very simply, people with a high self-esteem feel good about themselves and believe in their ability. Their appearance and body language means that people will treat them better and with more respect. You can dismiss this as claptrap if you wish, but the reality is that self-esteem is a very real and powerful force which determines, shapes and accelerates your success.

THE WINNERS IN LIFE TEND TO HAVE HIGH SELF-ESTEEM, WHILST THE LOSERS HAVE LOW SELF-ESTEEM

Good luck is an attitude of mind

If you toss a coin ten times and call correctly heads or tails, say, eight times, you have been lucky. But luck is a poor servant by itself, because sooner or later luck tends to even out. If you toss a coin 10,000 times you will only call correctly about 50% of the time, because statistically that must happen.

Some people are lucky in life, however, because they consciously put themselves in situations which are likely to be favourable. A phrase I use to describe this trait is to deliberately swim with the tide of opportunity. For example, the industry sector you choose to work in will influence how lucky or not you will be:

- information technology, despite short-term downturns and outsourcing jobs to third world countries, offers well paid employment, promotion opportunities and scope for becoming self-employed or starting your own business

- steel making is likely to continue to suffer from rationalization, redundancy and cheap imports

- pharmaceutical industry wages and salaries are considerably higher than average

DELIBERATELY SWIM WITH THE TIDE OF OPPORTUNITY

- a profession such as architecture offers lower rewards for many people than say, accountancy or commercial law, and provides fewer career opportunities outside of the profession.

In a similar way, your choice of university or business school will affect the luck you enjoy in later life. The friends you make, the people you get to know and the alumni circle of a really top establishment are likely to make you luckier than a third rate alternative, even if the grade of degree achieved is the same.

Exploit your talents

Everyone has an innate talent for something! The problem is that some people allow themselves to be stuck in jobs they hate, and never identify and pursue the opportunities to exploit a talent or hobby which they really enjoy. It could become a part-time source of extra income, lead to self-employment or turn into your own business.

To prove it works, some real life success stories include:

- A keen home cook offered to cook dinner parties for people in their own homes so she did not need to provide her own equipment, which she could not afford, and then invested what she earned to buy the utensils she needed.

- A photography enthusiast started out by taking portraits of people in her own home and then did freelance commercial photography.

- A wood carver carved small animals and sold them in local shops, restaurants and pubs on a sale or return basis.

- A skilful curtain maker made curtains at home for friends initially, and then expanded using local small ads.

- An IT manager advertised personal computer training and trouble shooting in your home, charged at a set hourly rate.

In each of these cases, people started without any cash outlay, did not give up their jobs initially, and found satisfying self-employment, and worked hours which suited their lifestyle.

So ask yourself
what talent or hobby of mine can I exploit?

Regard disability as an unfair advantage

You may be disabled or have a disabled child or relative and be really angry that anyone could suggest it is an unfair advantage. Well, I am unrepentant. Most disabilities can only be improved a bit at best, but your mental attitude is the key to transform your life. You can choose the attitude of mind that this is the stimulus to achieve what you want; or adopt the outlook you could never do it or even be given the chance.

There is absolutely no benefit to you by being downbeat, negative or sorry for yourself. At best, you will be given sympathy, but you have to admit that is the last thing you really want. Stop even

IF THE OUTCOME WOULD BE DISASTROUS, TAKING THE RISK IS AN UNAFFORDABLE GAMBLE

mentioning your disability, get on with what you want to achieve and you will gain huge respect.

Yes, you will face difficulties, frustrations and setbacks and you may have to persist, persuade and cajole even to get the opportunity. Do not be deterred. People are on your side and want to give you the opportunity.

I find Douglas Bader a truly inspirational example. An ace pilot in the second world war who lost his legs, but resumed his career with artificial limbs.

It is not being flip or offensive to describe disability as an unfair advantage. Your mental attitude, which is your choice, can turn it into an unfair advantage for you because you will have the determination, self-belief and persistence to achieve the success you want.

Assess the upside and downside of risks... always

Many people do not understand risk, including successful business executives and entrepreneurs who should know better. Risk can ruin your success, or severely undermine it.

It is easy to dismiss the risk because the possibility of a mishap is utterly remote and improbable. This misses the point completely. You have to ask yourself if the risk materializes, will it be disastrous, damaging or affordable. If the event would be disastrous, then following this route is an unaffordable gamble.

Let me illustrate this with a sad case I read in a newspaper. An executive in the financial services industry, which is highly regulated in order to protect the public, was convicted of travelling on the metro without a ticket. The regulators barred him from working in the industry. A personal disaster. It could be described as forgetful, mindless, reckless or just plain stupid. The probability of being caught and convicted must have been extremely low at that time. If caught, the overwhelming likelihood would have been a reprimand or a fixed penalty fine on the spot, but the consequences of a conviction make the risk absolutely unacceptable.

The meaning of risk-taking should be quite clear by now. If the outcome would be disastrous, taking the risk is an unaffordable gamble.

Another kind of risk people take is of not being found out, when the consequences would be disastrous. People do this in their personal lives by assuming that their marital infidelity will not be found out, probably knowing that it would end their marriage. Business people take similar risks knowingly. One company developed a range of exclusive designs for a major retail chain and the contract precluded copies or variations being sold elsewhere. Although the customer accounted for more than 16% of turnover, the managing director sold very similar designs to another retail chain assuming they would not be found out. They were found out almost immediately and lost their most important customer.

Always assume that you will be found out, and never take the risk that you will not be, if the result would be disasterous or damaging.

If any risk would be damaging, but not disastrous, then it is vital that you have a deliverable contingency plan.

A specialist printing company relied heavily on a pharmaceutical customer. The owner personally looked after the customer and the account grew. The sales director resigned, and it was decided to simply rely on the remaining sales person because new business was not a priority as the capacity was nearly fully utilized. Then the unthinkable happened. The pharmaceutical company was acquired and the account was lost because of supplier rationalization. Suddenly, the business was operating at a loss rather than being highly profitable.

There was no contingency plan. Worse still, the ability to win new customers had been knowingly depleted. The message should be clear, undue dependence is a risk, whether it is on a customer, a supplier or even a key employee. The counsel of perfection is to avoid undue dependence happening, but it tends to happen gradually. When undue dependence does happen, however, then every effort should be made to minimize the risk by taking positive action.

ALWAYS ASSUME THAT YOU WILL BE FOUND OUT

Smart people will assess the gains and rewards, the upside, but pay even more attention to assessing the downside risk in terms of:

- What could go wrong?
- What would be the consequences?
- What can we do to avoid or minimize the risk?
- What will we do if it happens?

Respect people and beware arrogance

It is entirely possible to become seriously wealthy, but fail to treat people with respect and become arrogant. These people are likely to treat those who serve them badly, such as taxi drivers and waiters, presumably because they look down on them. Yet they will treat successful people with respect.

Some successful business people treat their own staff badly, and occasionally atrociously. There is no benefit or justification what-soever for this, and the likelihood is that the person could have been demonstrably more successful by treating people with respect.

Your watchwords need to be to treat everyone you meet with:

- courtesy
- respect and
- charm.

As the world seemingly becomes ever more aggressive and competitive, courtesy and respect really stand out. And you will delighted with the beneficial results demonstrable charm brings.

UNDUE DEPENDENCE IS A RISK, WHETHER IT IS ON A CUSTOMER, A SUPPLIER OR EVEN A KEY EMPLOYEE

Key point summary

1 identify what is letting you down or holding you back

2 consciously translate your dreams into conviction, unshakeable belief and reality

3 identify and focus on the jugular vein of opportunity for you

4 rehearse your future success daily

5 develop your self-esteem

6 become lucky by swimming with the tide of opportunity

7 exploit your innate talents and hobbies to become wealthier and happier

8 regard disability as the stimulus to achieve what you have always wanted

9 identify and assess possible risks, if the outcome would be disastrous do not pursue it

10 create your own supporters club by treating everyone with respect, courtesy and charm

11 pursue your own personal action plan using the following page.

Personal action plan – mental outlook and approach to life

Date _____

I commit to the following action because I know it will make me wealthier and happier. I will change my mental outlook and approach to life as follows:

ACTION 1

ACTION 2

ACTION 3

ACTION 4

ACTION 5

3 Do yourself some valuable favours

THERE IS A POSITIVE ACTION you can and should take to build the solid foundations which will inevitably make you wealthier and happier. You will already be doing some of these to varying degrees, but this is not enough. You need to consciously work at all of them until they become an enjoyable conscious and sub-conscious habit. The deliberate action you need to take includes:

1 meet and learn from the rich and influential

2 network seriously

3 become image conscious and invest in your appearance

4 develop your charisma and poise

5 improve your skills and qualifications

6 find a rich life partner, if you are single

7 create a will

8 commit to a personal action plan

Each of these will be considered separately.

Meet and learn from the rich and influential

Many people regard a request for advice as a personal compliment, and will go out of their way to help. This is your powerful key to meet and learn from your own heroes.

At the age of 28, I wrote to my hero, the late Lord Weinstock of GEC, requesting to meet him for some career advice because my ambition was to become a managing director. He sent a most charming reply asking me to let his secretary know when would be a suitable time for me to visit him!

He was equally charming when we met and his advice included:

- make sure you are financially skilled before you become a managing director and consider qualifying as a management accountant in your spare time (which I did)
- get varied operational experience, do each job outstandingly well, and you will be given the opportunity to be a managing director.

You should consider identifying a few of your personal heroes and write them a carefully crafted letter designed to persuade them to meet you. Think carefully about whom to meet and your purpose. If you want to become a captain of industry or to build a business empire from scratch, choose accordingly.

If you are an ambitious career executive, identify three or four relevant firms of headhunters and find out which person is most appropriate for you to meet. Your aim should be to become known and get valuable career advice. Make it clear that you are not seeking another job at present and would value their observations on:

- how realistic your career goals and timescales are
- what gaps in your experience, skills or qualifications need to be addressed

- what type of job you should be aiming at next
- which market sectors you should consider for your next move
- companies they regard as excellent employers.

Having met headhunters, keep in touch with them and make sure they are kept informed of your career progress.

Network seriously

Networking is one of the most overworked and abused words of the decade, everyone claims to be on the bandwagon. It is a powerful tool which may produce the very opportunity you want, but too many people regard networking as simply collecting a business card from everyone they meet and filing the details in their contact database.

Serious networking needs to be targeted and sustained. Targeting means identifying and researching which events, clubs and associations you should attend. Possibilities include:

Local business clubs – probably worth finding out the number of members and their membership profile before attending

Networking events – hosted by national newspapers, organizations for directors and such like, likely to include a speaker or mini-conference

MBI clubs – regular events attended by people seeking to join management buy-in teams, as well as private equity houses and professional advisers

CONSIDER IDENTIFYING A FEW OF YOUR PERSONAL HEROES

Trade associations – dinners and project groups

Professional bodies – special interest group meetings

Alumni associations – such as schools, universities, business schools and former employers.

DEVELOP AND SUSTAIN A RAPPORT WITH THE PEOPLE YOU HAVE TARGETED

Scores of people, or even hundreds, may attend some events and you will manage to meet only a few of them. Further targeting is needed. At the event, scan the attendees and make an imperceptible beeline for those who appear to be the most influential.

Even so, there is no guarantee you will meet the most relevant people. Always obtain an attendance list, even if you have to cajole someone after the event. You can then select whom you wish to meet and telephone them to make contact.

Nowadays people receive so many emails, that the medium has become devalued. (Curiously, a letter has much more impact today because people receive so few of them.) Exchanging emails is simply not enough to develop a worthwhile relationship from networking.

You need to develop and sustain a rapport with the people you have targeted. Informal meetings and telephone conversations are needed, but time is your scarcest resource so you must select whom to focus upon.

Charity work could provide really valuable networking opportunities for you, and be a worthwhile and enjoyable leisure activity. Needless to say, you should search for high profile events and organizations. Quite often, the organizing committee consists of wealthy and successful people, but they need willing helpers to do some of the mundane work.

CREATING AN EFFECTIVE IMAGE IS ABOUT ATTENTION TO DETAIL

Please remember that I never promised quick and easy, gimmicky short-cuts, but valuable relationships with influential people often result from charity work.

Become image conscious and invest in your appearance

As outlined earlier, people treat you and respond differently according to your appearance because they react instantly and instinctively, at both a conscious and unconscious level. Television documentaries have demonstrated ample proof by changing the appearance of people to highlight the different treatment received.

Your appearance should reflect your future ambition today, it is not enough to be dressed consistent with your present position. If you become a top executive and wear quirky and outrageous neckties, people are likely to accept it as eccentricity. Conversely, if you are a junior manager similar neckties may be viewed adversely by the senior executive you rely on for promotion.

This is not a recipe for dull conformism. You should develop a personal style which will contribute to achieving your goal and not militate against it. Creating an effective image is about attention to detail. The basics do matter, your hair needs to be well groomed and fingernails impeccably clean. Your shoes need to be in good repair and always well cleaned – scruffy shoes are enough to under-mine an otherwise suitable image. Likewise, a silly fun watch or a half chewed plastic ballpoint pen detracts disproportionately.

One way to improve your image is to read fashion magazines and visit expensive clothing shops, even if you cannot afford to shop there at present you will get ideas. Some major department stores offer the services of a personal shopper, free of charge, and you are likely to get some good advice.

Image consultants are used by wealthy people to get a complete makeover, but the cost will rule this out for most people.

Develop your poise and charisma

Poise and charisma are elusive qualities, yet easily recognizable in others, and highly desirable. There is no doubt whatsoever, however, that:

You can develop *your* poise and charisma.

A good way to start is by observing people who display poise and charisma and understanding how they behave. Arguably, poise requires that you:

- are at ease in the situation you are in
- are in control of your emotions and thoughts
- you appear relaxed and calm
- you never flap.

A simple thing you can do is to give yourself time. If you arrive late for a business meeting or a dinner party, you are starting off on the back foot. Arrive in suitable time, avoiding any panics en route, so that you have a few moments to become relaxed and calm before making your entrance.

Adequate time gives you the opportunity to prepare for an unfamiliar situation, so that you will not be wrong footed. Some examples will illustrate the point:

- When attending a client or prospective client meeting, especially for the first time, find out from your team leader what contribution is expected from you and any traps you need to avoid.

- When speaking in public, arrive in sufficient time to familiarize yourself with the room, the position you will be speaking from and any equipment you will be using. Find out how you will be introduced, to avoid the chair inadvertently embarrassing you at the outset.

- When attending a drinks event, business or social, walk into the room confidently and approach anyone who is standing alone. They will be delighted to talk to you. Otherwise, look for just two or three people together and join them. If you stand looking lost, you are demonstrating a lack of poise.

Charisma is even more elusive than poise, but you can develop the traits which add up to charisma. It starts with your face and demeanour, your face should be friendly and your bearing confident and upright. On meeting someone, a warm smile, eye contact and firm handshake, or a confident kiss on the cheek in a social situation, are important.

Develop the habit of regarding contact with people or attending a meeting as a performance in which you will consciously switch into charismatic mode, and eventually it will become a sub-conscious habit. The word 'performance' does not imply any insincerity what-soever, but recognizes that you need to switch on your charisma from idling mode when you are with people.

Traits which add up to charisma include:

- an open stance
- demonstrating a genuine interest in the people you are with and giving them your undivided attention
- listening positively, not passively, to what they have to say
- giving something about yourself, without monopolizing the conversation or interrupting someone
- displaying impeccable manners and demonstrable charm
- have some interesting things to talk about (even if you have thought about possible things to say in advance) because this makes you interesting to other people
- exude vitality, energy and self-confidence in an understated way.

Improve your skills and qualifications

You may feel let down or missing out because of a lack of skills or qualifications. Whatever the reasons, you can change things. There has never been more opportunities to develop new skills and qualifications, using the internet, distance learning and part-time study as well as full-time courses.

You have the chance to reinvent your life and to do what you have always wanted. The possibilities are limitless. You may enjoy cooking but need the self-confidence of a cookery course to become a home dinner party cook for people. An army person retired in his thirties, and financially supported by his working wife, qualified as a lawyer and became a solicitor in general practice. A patent agent financed

YOU CAN FALL IN LOVE WITH A RICH PERSON JUST AS MUCH AS SOMEONE WHO IS POOR

herself for a full-time photography course and became a freelance photographer. An accountant, with a flair for interior design, took a course, set up in business and made her dream come true.

Find a rich life partner (if you are single)

You may find the very notion contentious or even offensive, after all you are romantic enough to choose a partner whom first and foremost you really love. I agree entirely with you, but argue that you can fall in love with a rich person just as much as someone who is poor.

If your social life centres on your local bar, visiting football matches and playing competitive darts, the overwhelming likelihood is that your partner will be poor. So if you have decided that to be richer and happier, you need to find a rich and influential partner give yourself every chance, for example:

- join an elite fitness club or really upmarket sports club
- take an interest in a sport such as polo
- drink in exclusive bars renowned for attracting the rich and famous
- become a member of a suitable members only club.

You must regard the expense involved as your personal investment, in the same way that an entrepreneur would invest in starting a business.

Create a will

You may feel this is an absolute contradiction. You want to enjoy your money, and when you die it is too late. Well it is, but in an entirely different way.

FIND OUT HOW TO LESSEN THE INHERITANCE TAX BURDEN

If you die without leaving a will, there are strict rules for the division of your estate which may be very different from what you want. Also, by the time you know you are dying, it is probably too late to mitigate inheritance tax.

So, don't put off creating a will, do it now and take the opportunity to find out how to lessen the inheritance tax burden. Then review your will as a matter of routine every five years to reflect any changes in your personal circumstances and the inheritance tax rules.

Commit to a personal action plan

Avoid the temptation to feel that you knew everything in this chapter and are already following the advice to varying degrees. That approach will not make you one jot richer or happier.

Write down and commit what you will do more of or differently, using the following action plan.

Do yourself some valuable favours
– personal action plan

Date _____

Meet and learn from the rich and influential

Networking

Personal image

Poise and charisma

Skills and qualifications

Find a rich partner

Key point summary

1 get expert career advice by meeting captains of industry and headhunters

2 invest time in targeted networking, and consider involvement in high profile charity projects

3 invest money in your appearance so that you already look the part you want to achieve

4 develop the traits which people recognize as poise and charisma

5 (if you are single) set out to find a rich and influential life partner

6 create a will to protect your wealth from avoidable taxes and to direct who will benefit

GIVE YOURSELF TIME
IF YOU ARRIVE LATE FOR A BUSINESS MEETING OR A DINNER PARTY, YOU ARE STARTING OFF ON THE BACK FOOT

4 Become richer with spare time opportunities

IF YOU WANT TO BE richer, whether you are in full-time employment, a single parent with children or whatever your status, making some spare-time to create wealth offers real opportunities which you cannot afford to ignore.

These can be classified as follows:

Proven opportunities
- your home
- tax free savings
- pensions, yes, pensions

Investment opportunities
- stocks and shares
- residential and commercial property
- precious metals
- art and antiques
- fine wines
- miscellaneous

Risky opportunities
- over-borrowing
- gambling
- spread betting
- day trading
- derivatives, warrants and contracts for difference
- get rich quick schemes

Each of these will be considered separately

Proven opportunities

These opportunities are described as proven (but categorically not guaranteed – especially within the short to medium-term), because the chances are high that these will make you richer in the long-term.

Your home

Your home was mentioned in Chapter 1 as a possible short-term way of becoming richer, provided that the housing market is favourable. Whilst past performance is never ever a reliable guide to future performance, your home is probably the best 'proven' opportunity over the long-term. From time to time, house prices drop sharply, but over either a 10 or 25 year period, house prices have consistently outperformed inflation.

YOUR HOME IS PROBABLY THE BEST 'PROVEN' OPPORTUNITY OVER THE LONG-TERM

So your long-term strategy should be to accumulate serious capital by developing the homes you live in. If you are competent at D-I-Y even better, but even if you are hopeless you can still profit by using local trades people to carry out the work.

If you believe your present home offers scope for profitable development, put your ideas to the test. Ask three estate agents to value your property and get their advice on what alterations and extensions would increase the value, compared to the costs involved. They may be able to tell you the price obtained for a house in your street which has been modified along the lines they have suggested.

A key to valuation is the number of rooms in the property. Adding a bedroom, a bathroom or a garage is likely to add net value, whereas turning two small rooms into say, a larger bedroom may reduce value. Expensive and indulgent makeovers of a kitchen or bathroom are likely to exceed the added value.

If your present home does not offer scope for development, consider buying a house with development potential. The keys to success include:

- understanding the local market
- position, position, position
- detailed cost estimates and control
- a realistic timescale.

ALWAYS EVALUATE THE DOWNSIDE RIGOROUSLY AND HAVE DELIVERABLE CONTINGENCY PLANS TO COPE EFFECTIVELY WITH THE UNEXPECTED

You need to research the immediate market area to understand the type of buyer that the house will attract after development. Avoid uninformed assumptions and get free advice from local estate agents.

If residents are primarily couples with young children the local amenities and property features which are relevant will be quite different from the successful single executive. Ignore your likely buyer at your peril. Priorities for a family with young children include pre-school nurseries, schools, room for the children to play, and an eat-in kitchen may be popular. The single executive will be attracted by nearby restaurants, bars, a fitness club, ease of commuting and a small kitchen may well be entirely acceptable.

Ask local estate agents if they are selling any houses they consider ripe for redevelopment and find out how they would add value. Whichever way you find your property, always use estate agents for advice on features that will add value and the market value today if the property had already been developed.

Position, position, position is an overworked phrase, trite and certainly true. It is the thing you cannot change or improve much. An adjacent busy road will be a minus for parents with young children, and proximity to a railway or metro station will be important to young executives.

Other factors to be wary of include persistent noise from trains, aeroplanes or heavy traffic; pressure for a by-pass which could affect the property sooner or later, an outlook marred by an eyesore and so on.

Detailed cost estimates and subsequent cost control determine the profitability of the development even when you have made a sound decision on the property to buy. Mental guesstimates are totally inadequate; a written and itemised budget, with a contingency of about 15% of the total project cost, is essential.

Visit do-it-yourself stores to get specific information on the cost of materials and appliances. Contact two or three small builders to get informal estimates for any work you need to have done before you make the decision to buy. This may sound a counsel of perfection, but it should prevent expensive mistakes. Invest in a survey of the property to find out if there is a hidden problem such as subsidence or severe damp before you buy. The survey cost should be included in the budget, together with interest costs on any loan you take out to finance the renovation work, the legal costs and agency fees for buying and selling the property.

A sensible timescale is essential. If your financial situation requires that you have renovated the property and sold it within, say, six

OVER, SAY, A
20 YEAR PERIOD
IT IS POSSIBLE TO CREATE A VALUABLE AND PORTABLE FUND WHICH YOU COULD USE TO CREATE YOUR OWN PENSION

to nine months you are taking a risk. Renovation work often takes longer than expected and anyway, do you really want to be on an exhausting treadmill, without any social life for several months? In the meantime, the housing market may unexpectedly plummet preventing you from selling at a profit. What happens if you are made redundant?

As outlined in Chapter 2, always evaluate the downside rigorously and have deliverable contingency plans to cope effectively with the unexpected.

You may feel that my doom and gloom is enough to put you off property development for life. Absolutely not! The purpose has been to make you aware of the pitfalls in order to maximize your chances of success and motivate you to continue with successive development projects which fit into your chosen lifestyle and make you richer. Once you have developed your home fully, consider selling it and buying another one which is ripe for profitable development.

Tax free savings

Tax free savings will make you a bit richer but not rich, so they are no big deal. Nonetheless, you will be maximizing the gain from your chosen investment, which is an important habit to develop. In the UK, you can invest several thousands a year, free of both income and capital gains taxes, either in a deposit account earning interest or in stock market investments. Over, say, a 20 year period it is possible to create a valuable and portable fund which you could use to create your own pension.

> **A PENSION CAN BE A VEHICLE TO ALLOW YOU TO RETIRE EARLY AND GIVE YOU THE FREEDOM FROM WORK YOU REALLY WANT**

Pensions, yes, pensions

Boring! Risky! These may be your reactions to the notion of pensions.

If you are in your twenties, even thinking about pensions may be anathema to you. Wrong; a pension can be a vehicle to allow you to retire early and give you the freedom from work you really want.

Take full advantage of your employer's pension scheme, even if you are required to match the contribution made by the employer. The build up of a substantial pension refund requires the long-term compounding effect of gains. By putting off investment into a pension fund, the reality is that you may never be able to invest enough to recover the lost ground.

Risky is an accurate description many people would use who have invested in pension funds and suffered the damaging effects of financial scandals. Today it is possible to create your pension fund in the UK in the form of a SIPP, a Self Invested Personal Pension. It is effectively an inexpensive 'wrapper' in which to put your own investments. Up to the annual contribution limit which is age related, you benefit from tax relief at your highest level and a pension can be drawn from the age of 50, although the minimum age may be increased.

If you own a company, a SIPP can be used to buy business premises. The money in the fund can be used to purchase a property, which must not be already owned by you, the company or other shareholders, or the SIPP can borrow up to 75% of the property value. The company must pay a commercial rent to the SIPP and the sale of the property is free of capital gains tax in the fund.

A SIPP is equally relevant, however, to make equity investments. Your aim should be to build up a substantial fund value by the age of 50, so that you no longer need to earn an income. Consequently, it makes sense for the fund to be invested in a mix of safer investments, with a minority of riskier opportunities to add some spice.

Despite the bad press that pensions have received, a pension fund is a tax effective way to allow you to retire or only to work part-time by 50 with a continuing income.

Investment opportunities

The following opportunities have the potential to make you seriously richer, but there is always the risk of substantial losses. The key issues of spreading risk and your need for liquidity must be understood at the outset.

Spreading your risk is likely to materially reduce your potential losses, but it will also reduce your potential gains. If you were to invest in a single share, even a blue chip stock, there is the possibility that the share price could increase or decrease by 50%, even if the rest of the stockmarket is virtually static. If you spread your investment over 10 companies, the chances of making an overall gain or loss of 50% in a static market are extremely low. This is the rationale behind the popularity of mutual funds, unit trusts and other collective equity investments. If you believe that shares in the pharmaceutical and health industries look set for growth, seek out a fund which will give you the opportunity to invest in a spread of companies in the sector.

Your liquidity needs can affect the gain or loss you are likely to make. The investments in this section should be regarded as medium to long-term opportunities, because the need to sell may force you to crystallize a loss or cut short a potential gain. For example, you may decide to invest your holiday savings in the stock market for a few months. If the market has fallen temporarily, but you feel obliged to sell because your family really need a holiday, you may have to sell at a loss and find that twelve months later you could have realized a handsome gain.

Stocks and shares

For long periods during the second half of the twentieth century it was difficult not to achieve worthwhile gains on the stockmarket of your choice. Shares proved to be the most profitable investment opportunity. The early years of this century delivered widespread losses, and expectations are now much lower. Furthermore, a major terrorist attack or a worldwide epidemic could damage share prices worldwide and recovery would take time, so stockmarket investment should not be rejected but a healthy dose of realism is required.

Your choice of where to invest is of the essence. When stockmarkets are under-performing, consider investing for dividends rather than concentrating on capital growth. Collective income funds have performed much better than capital growth vehicles under these difficult conditions.

Sensible investment decisions require you to evaluate the:

- countries
- sectors
- companies.

When Europe and the USA stock markets are declining, it is entirely possible that, say, Hungary or Thailand are enjoying a bull market. In these smaller markets, you may find an opportunity to invest in a fund concentrating only in a particular country. Once you have invested, however, monitor the share index for that country as the share price of your own investment in order to get an early warning of a falling market.

Within major stockmarkets, sector considerations are important. When the economic outlook is uncertain, defensive sectors could outperform the overall market. Public utility services, tobacco and defence shares may fall into this category. So look out for articles and websites commenting on defensive sectors. In larger stock-markets, collective investments focus on various different sectors so it may be possible to invest in your chosen sector without having to pick individual companies.

If you decide to invest in individual companies, do your homework first. Is there an unbroken record of consistent growth in sales and profits? Or has it been a roller-coaster ride for investors? Evaluate what the risk factors are. If the share price is bolstered by the hope of successful clinical trials of a major drug or commercial exploit-ment of new technology, recognize that failure or even significant delay could cause a sudden price plunge.

Some investors suffered damaging losses by investing in high-yielding corporate bonds, commonly known as junk bonds. The

NEVER EVER BUY SHARES AS A RESULT OF AN UNSOLICITED PHONE CALL GIVING YOU A HOT TIP WHICH IS ABOUT TO TAKE OFF

exceptional returns promised by some collective bond funds, which invested in companies such as Enron and World Com, should have been recognized as involving exceptionally high risk. It is a myth that bonds are generally safer than equities. Investment grade corporate bonds have delivered worthwhile returns, as have government bonds such as US Treasury or UK Gilts, in difficult market conditions. The fundamental point is underlying quality rather than the promise of spectacular returns.

Spreading your risk has already been covered in this chapter, but you need to be aware of other techniques and traps:

- use stop-loss limits
- lock in gains
- recognize a lack of liquidity in smaller company shares
- be wary of share tips
- avoid scams.

USING STOP-LOSS LIMITS

Using stop-loss limits is a way to limit your losses. Whenever you buy shares in a company, a unit trust or other collective investment, set a stop-loss limit, say 10% or 15% below the purchase price. When the price increases, move your stop-loss limit up accordingly, so you are 'protecting your paper gains'. The technique requires that when the price falls to your stop-loss limit, you sell and do not procrastinate. This requires more self-discipline than most people have, but if you follow it religiously your losses will be limited.

A KEY TO SUCCESS IS THE CHOICE OF PROPERTY AND LOCATION, LOCATION, LOCATION IS OF THE ESSENCE

Investors have a tendency to watch prices go down, convincing themselves that the share will bounce back. It may well do – eventually; but you need to recognize that the price of many shares and collective investments will fluctuate over a wide range in any twelve month period. The stop-loss technique is arbitrary, and is designed purely to limit your losses. It is entirely contrary to the approach of Warren Buffet, the legendary investor, whose approach has been to buy a share and hold it though thick and thin for the long-term.

LOCK IN GAINS

Locking in your gains is another arbitrary technique. Some people sell one half of their holding each time the price increases by 50%. It is another approach designed to ensure you avoid watching the share price rise and then continue watching your gains disappear before selling.

LACK OF LIQUIDITY IN SMALLER COMPANY SHARES

Smaller company shares are popular with investors, because there is always the possibility of investing in the next 'Microsoft' type success story. You need to recognize, however, that the percentage difference between the buy and sell prices of smaller company shares may be more than 10%, and worse still there could be times when the only way one can sell the shares is on a 'matched bargain' basis. Which means the broker has to find a purchaser willing to buy your shares.

BE WARY OF SHARE TIPS

Newspapers, investment magazines, tip sheets and the internet offer you plenty of tips. You need to realize, however, that by the time you attempt to buy the shares some people will have already invested and brokers will have marked up the price so that some of the potential gain has already been lost to you.

AVOID SHARE SCAMS

Never ever buy shares as a result of an unsolicited phone call giving you a hot tip which is about to take off. Over the years, I have received countless phone calls from New York and further afield locations. If you receive a call, just put the phone down. There have been many cases where the company does not exist or is a hopeless investment.

Residential and commercial property

Poor stockmarket performance in recent years has fuelled a boom in buy to let residential property investment. As with many other booms, naïve investors rush in and scams abound. Some people have lost money by responding to adverts offering a complete service of raising finance, buying properties and finding tenants. A typical claim has been the opportunity to acquire a million plus portfolio by investing less than £100,000. The reality has turned out to be expensive finance, miserable properties and a lack of tenants.

It is folly to imagine that, buy-to-let residential property investment is a get rich quick opportunity. It may be in a booming property market, provided that you sell before a sharp fall or collapse. If you believe that residential property investment is for you, it is best to regard it as at least a 10 year investment so that you have a good chance of making a decent capital gain.

A key to success is the choice of property and location, location, location is of the essence. Some people read that a particular town or city is a hotspot and plunge in. First-hand, or better still, an intimate knowledge of the local area is essential. An area of high employment, good transport links and relevant local amenities are important considerations.

Many investors understandably choose to invest in flats rather than houses, to avoid unwanted complications with overgrown and unsightly gardens. A new flat may seem attractive, but you have to be satisfied that the price will support a viable rent for you. Your aim should be that your rental income will cover your mortgage or loan repayments and the cost of maintaining the property.

Local letting agents are a valuable source of knowledge which will allow you to judge the likely rent of a property before you decide to buy it. Before letting, ensure the property is spic and span. If some refurbishment is necessary, choose robust and low cost fittings, hardwearing but inexpensive floor coverings and a neutral colour scheme.

Commercial property investment has performed well in recent years, but it must be recognized that an economic slump could make a property temporarily unsaleable and the tenant could go bust.

RECOGNIZE THAT PURCHASING FROM A GRADUATION SHOW OF A LEADING ART COLLEGE MIGHT JUST TURN OUT TO BE THE NEXT DAVID HOCKNEY, BUT EQUALLY COULD PROVE TO BE UNSALEABLE

Generally speaking, the stakes are higher for commercial property than residential investment. The ability to borrow against the property is lower, often a maximum of 70%, and because unit prices are higher there is less opportunity to spread the risk over several properties.

The quality of the tenant is essential. A multinational offers much more security than a private company. Edge of town redevelopment schemes, new road systems and the introduction of congestion charges

IF YOU DECIDE TO INVEST IN GOLD, BUY INGOTS BECAUSE JEWELLERY IS AN INDULGENCE NOT AN INVESTMENT

to reduce traffic levels could adversely affect your investment. So it should be approached with caution by do-it-yourself investors, and investing in a collective investment scheme will deliver a greater spread of risk and much better liquidity when you wish to realize your investment.

Art and antiques

In the previous decade, prior to writing this book, the Zurich – AMR Art & Antiques Index rose steadily by about a third. This performance was similar to the international stock market indices, but without a period of high growth followed by a sharp and sustained decline. This should not be interpreted that art and antiques are a risk free route to steady capital growth, however, you do get the bonus of enjoying your investment.

Investing in quality, with suitable provenance, is essential. Recognize that purchasing from a graduation show of a leading art college might just turn out to be the next David Hockney, but equally could prove to be unsaleable. A real risk inherent in investing in art and

AN ACQUAINTANCE OF MINE HAS A PRAGMATIC VIEW TO INVESTING IN WINE, HE ONLY BUYS WINE THAT HE CAN AFFORD TO REALIZE BY DRINKING IT IF NECESSARY!

antiques is that fashions do change, and this can have a marked effect on realizable value. Also art and antiques should be regarded as somewhat illiquid investments. In order to get the best price it may well be necessary to wait for an auction which will attract relevant buyers, and there is always the risk that the item will fail to achieve the reserve price.

As with any investment, do your homework. Read magazines and websites to choose a particular sector(s) for investment. Visit established dealers to get their advice and attend relevant auctions to gauge the level of interest. Equally, beware of asking a dealer simply to recommend pieces for you to buy until you have decided your investment approach. Otherwise you may discover years later that unattractive stock was dumped on you.

Precious metals

Gold is regarded as a safe haven investment in uncertain times. From the September 11, 2001 attacks to the time of writing, gold has risen by about 40%. It has to be said, however, that price movements in gold are often fickle and can be affected by hedge funds buying or selling in anticipation of dollar value movements, because gold is valued in US dollar terms. If you decide to invest in gold, buy ingots because jewellery is an indulgence not an investment.

Fine wines

With knowing repetition, quality is vitally important. The best returns have been achieved by top notch old world wines. Château-Lafite and Château-Margaux wines bought en primeur have doubled in value in the last five years.

Buying wines en primeur is something of a gamble, however, even though it helps to maximize the potential return. En primeur means buying wine whilst it is still in the barrel, and the vintage may not be as highly rated as expected. Also, you need to think in terms of holding the wine for about five years so it is a medium-term investment. Economic slump in a major wine buying market may mean that prices fall sharply. An acquaintance of mine has a pragmatic view to investing in wine, he only buys wine that he can afford to realize by drinking it if necessary!

Miscellaneous investments

Various possibilities exist from memorabilia to personalized car number plates. It is claimed that car number plates have doubled in value over the past 10 years.

Any such items should be regarded as medium to long-term opportunities, which may prove difficult to sell at an attractive price if you need to realize your investment quite quickly.

WHENEVER YOU BORROW TO INVEST IN PROPERTY OR TO START A BUSINESS, ALLOW YOURSELF AN ADEQUATE SAFETY MARGIN OF CASH TO PROTECT YOU AGAINST THE UNEXPECTED

Risky opportunities

Over-borrowing

Over-borrowing is risky! Examples include:

- Taking out a huge mortgage on your home and becoming unable to maintain repayments because of ill-health or job loss, which ends in the lender repossessing your home.

- Investing heavily in residential buy-to-let property when interest rates are low and subsequently interest costs accelerate sharply, tenants are in short supply and you have to sell property at a loss to meet your outgoings.

Protect your ability to meet mortgage repayments on your home by taking out a low cost insurance policy. Whenever you borrow to invest in property or to start a business, allow yourself an adequate safety margin of cash to protect you against the unexpected.

Gambling

Gambling is strictly for mugs!

And you may end up addicted! The 'house' takes a set percentage, so you are seeking to defy gravity. My advice is unbending. Only gamble the amount you can afford to lose without even a second thought. **Otherwise, don't gamble**.

Spread betting

Spread betting is exactly what the name implies – gambling! And you already know my views on gambling. Spread betting is especially risky because you can win or lose heavily. Spread betting allows you to gamble on the price movement in individual shares, stock-market indexes, currencies, precious metals and commodities such as coffee or sugar.

The three month spread of gold may be between £386.50 and £388.00, expressed as a spread of 3,865 and 3,880. If you bet that the price will rise about 3,880, and your stake is a dollar, pound or euro a point, and it rises to 4,000 you will win 120, free of capital gains tax in the UK. If you bet that the price will fall below 3,865, you will lose 135 if the price rises to 4,000.

Gains and losses are realized when you close the bet, which you can do at any time. Usually, spread betting firms offer a 'stop-loss' which closes the bet at an agreed price to limit your losses. I hope that you have been convinced that spread betting is gambling, and will not be tempted by adverts offering to teach you how to make handsome and regular income from spread betting in your spare time.

Day trading

Day trading involves buying and selling shares on-line, monitoring them continuously, and being ready to sell minutes or hours later in order to realize a tiny profit net of dealing costs. Some people do succeed in making a modest to reasonable annual profit, but individual months could deliver a loss. Arguably, day trading is not as potentially dangerous as spread betting, but is certainly speculative and most people would regard it as gambling.

Derivatives, options and covered warrants

No less a person than Warren Buffett described derivatives as financial weapons of mass destruction. This is fair comment when derivatives are used to gamble, but they can be used to protect your investments.

Derivatives allow you to bet on price movements of individual shares or stockmarket indexes without owning the asset. Options are a simple form of derivative. A call option gives you the right to buy a given number of shares at a set or strike price, by paying a fixed premium. A put option gives you the right to sell at the strike price. There is no obligation to buy or sell the shares under option, you can simply let it lapse at the end of the option period and your loss is the premium paid.

ALLOW YOURSELF AN ADEQUATE SAFETY MARGIN OF CASH TO PROTECT YOU AGAINST THE UNEXPECTED

If you have a call option to buy shares at £200 within the next three months, and the price rises to £250 by the time you sell, you have made a profit of £50 per share minus the cost of the option premium.

The main difference between an option and a future is the holder at the end of the future period must exercise it, so that if you bought the future to buy at £200 and the price falls to £150 you will have made a substantial loss. Futures can be traded, however, so that you can close your position and crystallize a gain or limit a loss.

If you anticipate that the price of a share you have invested in will fall significantly within the next three months, and selling would trigger a substantial capital gains tax liability, you could take out a put option. If the price does fall, then you have covered your loss for the cost of the option premium. If the price rises above the cost of the option, contrary to what you expected, you have made a net profit. So there is no doubt that derivatives do offer a cost effective way to protect the value of your shareholding against a sharp price fall.

Covered warrants are similar to options but are issued by investment banks rather than exchanges. Warrants are traded on stock exchanges and can be bought and sold through a stockbroker. Warrants have extended into oil, gold and commodities.

Get rich quick schemes

If it sounds too good to be true, it is!

This is an old adage, but one you can only ignore at your financial peril. Offshore bonds offering dramatically higher rates than other bonds, ostrich and llama farming, and other exotic investment schemes have repeatedly proven to be fraudulent and hugely speculative, and people have lost their entire investment.

Key point summary

1 develop your home to maximize value, sell and repeat the process to accumulate capital

2 understand investment risk: if the worst were to happen, even if it is improbable, can you afford the consequences?

3 buy-to-let residential property investment needs a measured approach and is not a licence to print money

4   if you invest in art, antiques or fine wines, always invest in the top quality available

5   gambling is for mugs: only gamble an amount you really can afford to lose without a second thought

6   recognize that spread betting, financial derivatives such as futures and options, and day trading are sophisticated forms of gambling where you can lose much more than expected

7   stay clear of get rich quick schemes and investment scams; always assume that if it looks to good to be true – it really is!

5 Get to the top... or higher than you thought possible

FOR MOST PEOPLE, CAREER SUCCESS is the key opportunity to becoming richer. Yet for many people work is just a treadmill, when it should be regarded as a major investment opportunity which needs managing carefully.

There is plenty you can do and traits you should develop to accelerate your career success, including:

1 be unswervingly honest, loyal and reliable

2 become a resultaholic not a workaholic

3 maximize your enjoyment and minimize stress

4 benefit from a mentor and coach

5 make yourself redundant or reinvent your role

6 think, talk and act strategically

7 be at IT's leading edge

8 sharpen your decision-making skills

9 demonstrate leadership

10 improve your financial know-how

11 invest in a world class MBA

12 really learn a second language

13 market yourself internally and externally

14 ask for shares or share options.

Each of these will be considered separately.

Be unswervingly honest, loyal and reliable

It is simply not enough to be honest, loyal and reliable most of the time. I am demanding that you are unswervingly honest, loyal and reliable, so I will explain just what is expected of you.

LOYALTY IS THE FOUNDATION OF TRUST

Honesty is more than not stealing from your employer, it is about intellectual honesty and acting with integrity as well. For example, if you are asked to meet a deadline which you feel cannot be achieved, or only by cutting corners, have the courage to say so at the outset and seek the help you need. If you have made a mistake, have the courage to admit it rather than stay silent in the hope it will not be discovered. I do not need to labour the point, but I can sum it up by saying always act impeccably.

RELIABILITY IS A VITAL QUALITY WHICH IS VALUED AT EVERY LEVEL IN ANY ORGANIZATION

Loyalty is the foundation of trust. Your immediate manager has a right to expect your loyalty and support from the outset. If you feel that he/she is not sufficiently supportive or is undermining your position, express your concerns at a suitable opportunity and seek a positive way forward. If you have reached the point where you are gossiping or complaining to colleagues about your manager, or worse still you are attempting to create disruption, either tackle the problem, seek a transfer or find a new employer.

Loyalty to your colleagues is equally important. Recognize that whenever you gossip about a colleague, people will recognize that they too will inevitably be the subject of your gossip behind their back. Any form of backstabbing of a colleague must be regarded as totally unacceptable, yet I believe it to be widespread. My message is unbending, be loyal and supportive of your colleagues or the reputation you gain will haunt you when you want and need the help and trust of those colleagues.

Reliability is a vital quality which is valued at every level in any organization. Develop the reputation that when you agree to do something by a deadline, it will be done well, and on time. In the unlikely event that a situation develops which may delay completion, always give advance notice and ask for the help and resources needed to meet the deadline.

LIKE ALCOHOLICS, MANY WORKAHOLICS ARE IN DENIAL

You may feel that my treatment of honesty, loyalty and reliability have been nothing short of patronizing. Nonsense! These traits are vitally important, and whilst we all like to believe that we rate highly, there is always scope for further improvement.

Become a resultaholic not a workaholic

Often, workaholics are not effective people, they are merely addicted to work. Few people can work effectively for more than 55 hours a week on a sustained basis. Like alcoholics, many workaholics are in denial.

20% OF THE TIME YOU SPEND WORKING DELIVERS 80% OF YOUR CONTRIBUTION

In addition to working excessive hours, tell-tale signs of a workaholic include regularly taking work home in the evenings and at weekends, or going into the office at weekends. Choose to become a resultaholic and you will achieve more, spend less time working, suffer less stress, improve family relationships and have more leisure time. The action required is simply to decide:

- which results and tasks are most important, and allocate the time and priority these deserve
- what can be left undone, tackled less often, or done by someone else
- those meetings you don't really need to attend, and can keep informed by reading the minutes
- to delete your name from unwanted reports and minutes
- to ruthlessly stop unwanted e-mails at source
- to decline unwanted lunch and dinner invitations.

In many jobs, 20% of the time you spend working delivers 80% of your contribution, so severely cut back on the less important tasks and you could save from 10 to 30 hours a week.

Maximize your enjoyment and minimize stress

STRESS THREATENS YOUR HEALTH AND MUST BE TACKLED PROMPTLY

Enjoyment at work is so important, yet probably only a minority of people regard their employment as enjoyable. If you work in a business sector which you dislike, for whatever reasons, get out as soon as possible and choose a career in a sector you will enjoy. If you really dislike the values and the culture of your company the same advice applies, get out as soon as possible. Unethical business standards, sexual harassment, bullying and such like are simply intolerable.

If you are happy with both the sector and your company, you may dislike your present job. Recognize that companies do not want to lose valuable staff, so talk to your immediate manager to initiate a request to obtain another job in the company.

Whilst there are some aspects of nearly every job which are not particularly enjoyable, do talk to your immediate manager in a positive way if there are parts of your job that you dislike. Do whatever it takes to maximize your enjoyment at work.

Stress is personal and subjective. You may find your job unacceptably stressful whilst your colleagues find the work stimulating. Do not suffer in silence. If the volume or type of work is stressful to you, talk to your immediate manager about reorganizing your job or an internal transfer. Stress threatens your health and must be tackled promptly.

Benefit from a mentor and coach

Top sportspeople such as athletes, golfers and tennis players rely heavily on a coach and mentor. They benefit from improved skills and mental attitudes. You may not realize it, but many successful business executives rely equally heavily on a mentor and coach. Furthermore, chief executives and entrepreneurs are just as likely to have a coach and mentor as younger, aspiring executives. Their companies are happy to pay for expensive coaching and mentoring because the company obtains worthwhile benefits. More importantly, you can have a mentor and coach committed to your personal success and development, free of charge.

Some companies are so committed to coaching and mentoring that every new employee is given one from within the company. If not, choose your own. Look out for a successful person in the company and, in a low key way, seek their advice. As a rapport develops, gradually build a coaching and mentoring relationship.

Your immediate manager may well attempt to be your coach and mentor, and this is to be welcomed, but there are potential conflicts of interest which may compromize the benefits for you. A previous manager you had in the company, however, may be a more suitable mentor because a conflict of interest is much less likely. Alternatively, your manager in a previous company may make an ideal mentor.

Other potential sources to find a mentor include someone you have met as a result of networking, or possibly a friend of your family. Some people look to a parent to be their career mentor, but I am not convinced this is appropriate. If ever a parent attempted to teach you how to drive a car, you will understand exactly what I mean.

Make yourself redundant or reinvent your role

Your immediate reaction may be that to make yourself redundant is nothing less than making yourself unemployed. Absolutely not! People with the rare insight and ability to make themselves redundant are highly valued.

PEOPLE WITH THE RARE INSIGHT AND ABILITY TO MAKE THEMSELVES REDUNDANT ARE HIGHLY VALUED

There may be a talented and ambitious member of your team whom you could coach and train to take over your job. It is important to sell the idea to your immediate manager at the outset and to obtain agreement that positive efforts will be made to obtain an internal promotion for you.

If there is no opportunity to make yourself redundant, it is always possible to reinvent your role so that you are making a more valuable contribution. Firstly, create some capacity to take on new tasks by delegating work or saving time. Then offer to take on some of the tasks carried out by your immediate manager, especially the ones he or she dislikes doing. In this way, seek to learn new skills and more varied experience.

IT CAN NEVER BE TOO EARLY TO UNDERSTAND AND LEARN ABOUT STRATEGY

Think, talk and act strategically

Chairmen, chief executives and company directors should think, talk and act strategically all of the time, but the truth is very few do so. Unfortunately, a strategic outlook is not acquired simply or quickly on appointment as a director. It takes years to develop and hopefully the newly appointed director has already spent several years consciously developing these skills.

It can never be too early to understand and learn about strategy as a prelude to beginning to think, talk and act strategically. External training courses, books, business management magazines and the internet provide plenty of opportunities to learn.

UNDERSTANDING ABOUT STRATEGIC ISSUES IS RELATIVELY EASY, BUT DEVELOPING THE INBUILT HABIT OF THINKING, TALKING AND ACTING STRATEGICALLY IS ANOTHER

What are some of the characteristics of strategy? Timescale is one; strategy involves taking a medium to long-term outlook and perspective. Equally important is to consider the issues and implications company-wide, and not merely address departmental or functional concerns. Another requirement is to address the external environment which the company will have to adapt to and succeed in, rather than be concerned solely with internal management issues.

Some of the aspects of the future external environment which need addressing include:

- Technology changes which will impact upon the way the industry sector operates, e.g. reducing hardware costs and dramatically greater reliability may mean that maintenance contracts are not renewed and instead the norm becomes never repair equipment but simply replace it with the latest model.

- Developments in information technology, e.g. the impact of e-commerce and m-commerce on corporate procurement and distribution channels.

- Environmental issues which could affect the ways and costs of doing business in some industry sectors.

- Regulatory and legislative changes, e.g. restrictions imposed on the food industry following worldwide outbreaks of BSE in cattle, which may be extended to other animal foods and poultry.

- Energy and raw material shortages, e.g. oil and electricity, even in the developed world.

- Skill shortages, especially to cope with new technologies.

- Social change, e.g. the increasing welfare and tax burden caused by the aging population in some countries.

- The impact of global mergers on supply and demand.

- The upheaval caused by a growing number of local wars and regional conflicts.

Understanding about strategic issues is relatively easy, but developing the inbuilt habit of thinking, talking and acting strategically is another. Thinking strategically requires evaluating change and new ideas not just in terms of the benefit and cost to your department, but thinking through what will be the consequences elsewhere in the company and overall will there be an acceptable benefit and financial return for the company and the shareholders. Talking strategically requires presenting and addressing changes and proposed investments in overall company terms, and demonstrating that you have considered likely changes in the external environment.

To act strategically requires the implementation of decisions which are of strategic importance to the future of the business. The first step is to identify decisions which don't necessarily have to be taken in the immediate future but when made will have a strategic impact. Some examples are as follows:

- A private company where the shareholders are reaching retirement and there are no members of the family to continue. A decision could be made to groom the business for sale in, say, two years time or to strengthen and develop the management team with a view to encouraging a management buy-out in due course.

- A listed group with some businesses which are either demonstrably non-core or destined to be low growth, which decides to make a series of divestments.

- A medium-sized accountancy firm which lacks strength in various specialist departments and decides to pursue a merger with a complementary firm.

- A company providing vending services for beverages only decides to extend their snack vending in order to maximize the potential of the existing customer base.

EFFECTIVE DECISION-MAKING IS VITAL FOR CAREER SUCCESS

Be at IT's leading edge

Developments in information technology will continue to have a massive impact on business. You can choose to benefit from the inevitable changes, by becoming an architect of change, or you may well become a victim and end up redundant.

To be at the leading edge, you need to:

- ensure that you become trained and skilled in every new software application introduced in your department
- volunteer for project teams or working parties to evaluate new equipment and software, particularly where the impact will be company-wide
- join manufacturer or software user groups to find out how other companies are exploiting technology
- keep abreast of new developments by reading specialist magazines and websites
- become an expert within your department, or better still company-wide, on some new software.

Sharpen your decision-making skills

Effective decision-making is vital for career success. At the operational level, a major decision requires that every one of the following steps is addressed rigorously:

- discover the core problem, not merely the visible or local symptoms
- identify alternative outline solutions, before falling in love with one or developing one in detail, and if appropriate encourage team members to brainstorm ideas

- evaluate in outline the benefits, cost, disadvantages and consequences of each alternative solution across the whole company, to ensure that knock-on implications are taken into account
- choose the preferred alternative and subject it to rigorous evaluation
- formulate the specification for any equipment, hardware and software to be procured
- obtain alternative quotations and evaluate the financial stability and after sales service of suppliers
- calculate the incremental cash flows from the project and carry out a discounted cash flow evaluation to demonstrate that the financial return is adequate
- prepare an implementation timetable, with individual accountability assigned to people
- monitor the benefits obtained and implement any corrective action required.

Arguably, however, the most important decisions to be made are those which do not need making!

Problems require that decisions are made and solutions implemented. Opportunities do not have to be pursued, even if people are aware of them. Spectacular success and stealing a march on competitors are the potential rewards.

Some examples of decisions which did not have to be made include:

- the launch of the first airline loyalty programme for frequent flyers, which was so successful that nearly every airline has followed suit
- the first vehicle manufacturer to make a massive investment in robots to reduce production costs
- the first supermarket chain to exploit their customer base by offering car insurance, personal loans and mortgages.

Even if your company is not innovative enough to be the first to launch a new initiative, there may still be a lucrative opportunity to launch an alternative and improved version quickly, rather than simply adopting a relaxed wait and see attitude.

The most difficult aspect of making a decision to exploit an opportunity is to identify the opportunity. So you need to consciously ask yourself which decisions could have a spectacular impact on your success.

Demonstrate leadership

You may feel that you have no opportunities to demonstrate your leadership qualities because you do not manage a staff of your own. However, there are invariably opportunities to lead. Consider the following examples:

- You are one of a small group of, say, engineers or research analysts who share a team assistant. To avoid conflicting priorities and to ensure that the assistant really is part of the team, you could suggest a weekly meeting of everyone to ensure priorities are agreed and the assistant understands what the team has to achieve.

- You have a full-time assistant but spend a lot of your time out of the office attending client meetings. You should develop the habit of a regular weekly meeting not only to discuss the work to be done in the coming week, but to address how to communicate and work together more effectively.

Leadership is hard to define in a meaningful way, but is something which people instinctively recognize as being effective or poor. The ingredients of effective leadership include:

- induction of new staff, making sure that people are welcomed, introduced to colleagues, and given the basic training and background required for their job

- involving the whole team in setting the future direction and goals

- encouraging people to come forward with ideas and improvements, and to challenge the status quo

- creating a climate whereby people raise their problems and concerns and fully expect them to be addressed

- ensuring that workloads and rewards are equitable within the team

- regularly saying 'thank you' for a job well done and giving praise whenever deserved

- adopting a coaching and mentoring style of management rather than the outdated approach of command and control

- providing opportunities for learning new skills, personal development and a broadening work experience

- creating a climate of integrity, respect for the individual, teamwork and fair play

- ensuring people have a shared and committed vision for future success.

Improve your financial know-how

Although people are the most valuable asset in any business, finance is the common denominator. Demonstrable finance awareness marks out a person as someone with potential for promotion. Financial knowledge ensures that your ideas are not shot down because they are unaffordable, and helps you to sell them and obtain approval.

A working knowledge of a profit and loss account and an understanding of a balance sheet are essential basic skills. Financial analysis skills used for decision-making are important.

Ask for the opportunity to attend a two or three day financial knowledge course, because most companies are keen to promote financial awareness. More importantly, immediately afterwards seek to apply your newfound knowledge. Get involved with finance staff in budgeting and the financial evaluation of projects and decisions, otherwise your knowledge will quickly waste away and be forgotten.

If your company is not willing to pay for financial training, you could buy a book or pursue a basic financial skills course using distance learning.

A WORKING KNOWLEDGE OF A PROFIT AND LOSS ACCOUNT AND AN UNDERSTANDING OF A BALANCE SHEET ARE ESSENTIAL BASIC SKILLS

Invest in a world class MBA

The MBA, Master of Business Administration, qualification comes in many guises. Full-time courses range from about 10 months to 2 years in duration. Part-time and block release courses abound to enable students to continue their job. Distance learning courses, often with occasional residential weekend study, are legion. Predictably, the rigour, career benefits and the respect of employers differ widely.

To pursue any MBA course is a major decision because of the cost and time involved. You need to be satisfied that the benefits you will gain are worthwhile. The potential benefits include:

ACHIEVING A MAJOR CAREER SHIFT

If you are a technical specialist, perhaps a qualified engineer, even your present employer may be reluctant to give you a general management role and other companies are less likely to do so. An MBA may well help you to achieve the career shift you want.

INCREASING YOUR CAREER EARNING POWER

Despite the vast increase in the number of MBA students, the qualification should prove to be a good financial investment.

THE PEOPLE YOU WILL MEET

Fellow students are likely to include kindred spirits and it is possible that you will find people who wish to join you in starting a business; and alumni events could provide excellent networking opportunities.

Rigorous analysis is needed in choosing the right MBA for you. Review web sites, paying particular attention to any subject specialization or industry sector bias, if relevant for you. The key to choosing an MBA course, however, should be the pursuit of quality and reputation. Check out league tables and the basis for ranking. Seriously consider taking an MBA overseas to widen your experience. Whatever the league tables reveal, Harvard Business School continues to offer a first class qualification and experience.

As part of your research, attend MBA Fairs, and talk to present and recent students. Find out in detail an analysis of the jobs obtained by graduates.

When to do an MBA is an important issue. To get the maximum benefit a few years of work experience are important and to regard an MBA merely as the immediate step after university graduation is inappropriate.

Occasionally, successful executives in their late thirties ask for my advice about taking an MBA. The benefits are more doubtful, and it may well be a lack of self-confidence and self-belief that are the real issues. Unless there is a commitment to return to work for the present employer, an attractive career opportunity afterwards may prove elusive.

A more sensible approach is probably to persuade your employer to pay for you to take a residential Advanced Management Programme for senior executives, likely to involve two or three months study, at a world class business school. Your aim should be to get a commitment in advance that you will return to take up a general management appointment.

Really learn a second language

Business is global nowadays, not just international. Fluency in a second language is demonstrable evidence that you have embraced this reality. Many people choose to learn either French or German, simply because they studied it at school. In terms of global trade, however, Spanish is arguably much more widely spoken.

Your employer may hold language classes or be prepared to pay for you to take lessons at a specialist language school. You need to recognize, however, that language training quickly wears off without practice. So seek every opportunity to practice your skills. Better still, seeks a transfer overseas and you will have a solid foundation for lifelong proficiency in the language of your choice.

Market yourself, internally and externally

In the current competitive business environment, every business markets their products and services to some degree. It is simply not enough to deliver the best product or service in your sector.

Outstandingly successful individuals market themselves, often eagerly paying a specialist agency to help them, because they know it is the route to success and wealth.

Tiger Woods, David Beckham and Catherine Zeta Jones have become brand names in their own right. They earn dramatically more than other people who are nearly as talented as themselves.

Yet very few business people consciously market themselves, even though it can dramatically accelerate your career success and earning power.

With your own company you should seek opportunities to join working parties and project teams which give you wider exposure within the company, especially to senior managers outside of your own department. Volunteer to speak at internal company training courses and conferences.

External marketing is even more important and provides many opportunities including:

- become active in your trade association or professional body and consider volunteering for an organizing committee role

- join an industry user group such as one organized by your IT supplier

- write an article for your trade press by telephoning the features editor to suggest one or two relevant topics and be sure to ask what they feel will be particularly interesting to their readers

- offer to speak at conferences by contacting the event organizer and remember that real life case study presentations are always welcomed

- contact relevant leading headhunters and ask for their career advice.

The message to you should be quite clear, do not rely on your ability alone but do showcase your talents to the widest possible audience.

Ask for shares or share options

If you work for a company that has a share option scheme, signal your keenness to benefit as part of your commitment to the company.

Even more important and potentially valuable, you may work for a private company which does not have a share option scheme – yet! Sound out the owner(s) about the opportunity to buy some shares or to receive some options because you wish to make a long-term commitment to the company. If you feel this may not be well received, consider asking one or more colleagues if they would like to join you in making a request.

Remember, if you do ask, you may receive, but if you don't it may never happen.

Key point summary

1 recognize that unswerving honesty, loyalty and reliability are highly valued

2 become a resultaholic and realize that 20% of your time may deliver 80% of the results you achieve

3 build enjoyment into your working life and take positive action to minimize stress

4 develop the habit of thinking, talking and acting strategically

5 demonstrate leadership qualities in everything you do

6 position yourself at IT's leading edge or risk becoming a victim of technology

7 market yourself within your company and externally to showcase your ability

8 ask for shares or share options if you believe your contribution deserves ownership participation.

THERE WAS ONLY ONE THING, WHICH DELAYED THEM GETTING STARTED

UNNECESSARY PROCRASTINATION

6 Become self-employed or start your own business

UNLESS YOU ARE A SENIOR executive with lucrative share options, self-employment or running your own business is likely to make you considerably richer than working for someone else. Furthermore, if you create a business which can be sold then you will exit with a substantial lump sum.

Even more important, self-employment or running your own business puts you in control of your working life, and for many people adds dramatically to their happiness.

Self-employment or starting your own business is neither an idle dream nor an impossible one, but an option potentially open to everyone.

To make sure that your dream becomes a reality, however, and not a living nightmare, you need a route map to ensure success and the essential steps include:

> 1   recognize that procrastination is your worst enemy

2   realize that opportunities are staring you in the face

3   mundane chores may be a route to success for you

4   test your idea in your spare time to minimize risk

5   develop the personal traits for success

6   acquire the essential skills for success

7   research your market and your competitors

8   write a convincing business plan to raise the finance you need

9   realize profit is important, but cash flow is life or death

10   decide when to cash in your chips

11   become a franchisee

12   buy an established business

Each of these issues will be considered separately.

Procrastination is your worst enemy

Don't you believe me? Well you should! Nearly everyone I have asked has said to me "You know I should have become self-employed or started a business years ago and with hindsight there was nothing to stop me". There was only one thing, which delayed them getting started – unnecessary procrastination.

Today may not be the best time to take positive action to become self-employed or to start a business, but unless your personal circumstances make it a nonsense, today is the best possible day.

Why? Simply because if you wait for a better time, or worst still the 'best' time, this may never materialize.

Opportunities are staring you in the face

The section *Exploit your talents* in Chapter 2 demonstrated how a hobby or an unexploited skill may provide the opportunity you seek. Examples included a keen home cook, an amateur photographer and a talented curtain maker. Self doubt is a self imposed obstacle. Any thought that you cannot be as goods as the 'professionals', namely people who are already self-employed or own a business, must be dismissed. If your friends tell you that you have a talent, this is proof enough that you are good enough.

An unskilled acquaintance hated his dead end job in a factory, but he really enjoyed cleaning his car and his friends commented just how meticulous he was. He was persuaded to ask a local upmarket public house if he could offer to clean cars for customers, and predictably the publican became his first customer. Almost overnight he had found profitable and enjoyable weekend work.

IF YOUR FRIENDS TELL YOU THAT YOU HAVE A TALENT, THIS IS PROOF ENOUGH THAT YOU ARE GOOD ENOUGH

One customer suggested he placed adverts in local newsagents windows offering to clean and valet cars at home. Once again, more work quickly materialized and a customer asked if he would visit his company every week to clean the fleet of company cars. Today, he has a successful business and employs two other people as car cleaners.

A marketing executive was made redundant in his early fifties and failed to get another job. So with his executive car that he bought from his employer on leaving, he decided to set up a chauffeuring service because he really enjoyed driving. In fact, he enjoyed marketing his own business even more and today employs several other drivers.

Mundane chores are a route to success

As discretionary spending power increases, people are looking for help to organize their life, do chores for them and save them time. If you do not believe me, ask lots of people what help they value most and what help they wish was available or is difficult to find.

Expect to be amazed at the list of possibilities which will arise, because they are so mundane and should be obvious including:

- a collect and deliver ironing service
- hedge trimming
- patio laying
- clothes tailoring and repairs ·
- garden shrub pruning
- interior design

- PC/laptop training
- yoga lessons at home
- dinner party cooking
- birthday and wedding cake making
- lawn cutting
- a handy person for odd jobs
- turf laying
- car maintenance at home
- window cleaning
- fence replacement and repair
- garden design
- music lessons for adults
- organizing children's' parties.

Test your idea in your spare time

If you are to become successfully self-employed or own your own business, minimizing risk needs to be a creed that you adopt at the outset and always pursue.

Your aim must be to make money in double quick time. Launch your venture at minimal cost. An advertising card in a local newsagents shop, a small advert in a church magazine or a low cost handbill delivered by you is all that is needed to get started. Avoid the temptation to buy expensive specialist equipment. Use

PASSION IS A VITAL INGREDIENT FOR BUSINESS SUCCESS

what you already own, even if it is not particularly efficient or suitable; and if you really need to buy, do hunt around for second-hand bargains.

You do not need to form a limited liability company, yet it is surprising how many people get carried away with the ego trip of being a director of their own company. This can come later when the success achieved justifies the expense involved.

Even more important, do not take the risk of giving up your present job until you are satisfied that your venture will quickly provide you with an acceptable income.

Your aim must be that if the venture fails, or is simply much less successful than expected, you can close it down at minimal cost. In this way, you will be ready to pursue an alternative opportunity and learn from the experience you have gained.

Personal traits for success

You should assess your suitability for going it alone in terms of the following personal traits based on management research and interviews undertaken by various institutions, journalists and gurus.

The most important personal traits for success include:

- **Hunger**

  You need to be hungry for success and there is absolutely nothing wrong with a burning hunger to be wealthy. Evidence of the requisite degree of hunger includes single-mindedness, focus, high ambition and demonstrable commitment. Many people find the description of driven to be an unattractive label, but it is another sign of real hunger.

- **Passion**

  Passion is a vital ingredient for business success. A passion to offer the best possible product or service at a competitive price. A passion to deliver outstanding customer service. A passion to get every detail right for your customer. A passion to exceed every customers expectations. A passion which turns every customer into an ambassador for your business. A passion to motivate, develop and reward your staff. A passion not just to be the best but to be recognized as the best. A passion for... I hope you have the message... a passion for every aspect of your business.

- **Resilience**

  Self-employment and your own business are littered with setbacks, unexpected problems and delays. Robert the Bruce may have tried several times to succeed, but you need to be ready to make him look like a premature quitter. You need to exhude the can do – will do approach. Whatever the setback you can and will overcome it. Even if your major customer goes bust or your premises are burned down, you will bounce back in double quick time.

- **Flexibility**

  Your job is to do whatever needs doing, even if some tasks are boring and menial, to ensure success. Your attitude must be to experiment, to be innovative, to do things differently. The only status quo you should tolerate is not to have one. Never be complacent enough to say 'this is the way we do things' but always add 'but only until we can find a better way'.

- **Competitiveness**

  Winning isn't the only thing, winning is everything. You cannot be content because you are winning a higher percentage of pitches for new business than your competitors. If you lose a pitch, find out why and learn from losing, but better still persuade your prospective customer or client to change their mind.

You may be inclined to dismiss the above traits as something which everyone has to a differing degree. You are absolutely right in one sense, but the whole point is that the successful go-it-alone business person needs to have these qualities in abundance and to consciously develop them.

Skills needed for success

As well as important personal traits for success, there are fundamental skills which are common to virtually every business. These are:

- selling
- marketing and
- financial awareness.

If you are to become successful, you need to develop your skills in each of these areas.

SMOOTH TALKING AND THE ABILITY TO TELL JOKES HAVE GOT NOTHING TO DO WITH SELLING

YOUR OWN PASSION, BELIEF AND ENTHUSIASM FOR YOUR PRODUCT OR SERVICE ARE A POWERFUL SELLING TOOL

Selling

The ability to sell is absolutely vital for your success, not just to sell your product or service but to get what you want from suppliers, your bank manager and your own staff.

Some people wrongly imagine that selling is unprofessional and anyway they could never be a salesperson, which is nonsense. Smooth talking and the ability to tell jokes have got nothing to do with selling.

The key to selling a product, a service or an idea is asking questions, and carefully listening to the answers. Questions allow you to find out what your prospective customer wants or needs and to learn their objections to placing an order. Then your job is to demonstrate how you can deliver what they want and overcome their objections.

Recognize that people buy the benefits of a product or service, not the specification. Car sales executives often wax lyrically about the engine technology and specification. A much more effective technique it to ask the prospective customer what are the most important features for them. If the answer is performance, then acceleration, cornering, a sports driving mode option and superior

THE MOST EFFECTIVE MARKETING PROMPTS PROSPECTIVE CUSTOMERS TO CONTACT YOU

braking are the features and benefits of interest, not the engine specification. On the other hand, the customer may say that the in-car entertainment sound system is really important and the engine is of little concern.

Your own passion, belief and enthusiasm for your product or service are a powerful selling tool. Your own customers are a powerful sales tool for you as well. Always ask them for either a testimonial, which you can post on your website, or to agree to be telephoned by a prospective client as a reference. Similarly, be ready to ask individuals if they can give you contact details of family and friends which may be prospective customers. Ask corporate customers if they can introduce you to other departments, other subsidiaries or their friends in other companies.

Closing the order or sale is of the essence. You must always be ready to seize the moment and ask for the order. If the answer is "I need time to think about it before making a decision" this is a clear signal that they have hidden or unstated objections. Ask more questions to find out the remaining objections, address them and be ready to ask for the order again. If you let the person escape, you may well have lost the sale.

I hope that by now you are convinced you can sell effectively and are motivated to learn more by visiting websites or buying a book.

Marketing

Every business can benefit from marketing, ranging from a well designed postcard advert placed in a newsagents window, to press advertising, website design and direct mail shots to a sophisticated public relations campaign.

The purpose of marketing is to make a wider, and relevant, audience aware of your business products and services. The most effective marketing prompts prospective customers to contact you but at the very least it pre-sells your business so that prospective customers are already aware of you before you contact them.

Your local newspaper may be a great and free marketing opportunity for you. My newspaper carried a feature on two women who had launched a collect and deliver ironing service and ended by giving their telephone number. All it takes is the imagination to telephone a journalist to sell the business idea that is worthy of a feature.

You simply cannot dismiss marketing and you must realize that there are techniques which work. Once again, visit websites and buy a book. For example, find out what techniques work for a direct mailshot campaign before you spend your money.

Financial awareness

Most major banks produce free business start-up guides. Inexpensive paperback books are devoted to start-ups and websites offer help. You may feel it is a counsel of perfection to say you should have done this before you start in business, but you can never do it soon enough.

Filing receipts, maintaining records, paying employee taxes and suchlike need to happen from the outset.

Research your market and your competitors

You should not start self-employment or a business on a hunch or gut feeling alone. A do-it-yourself approach is needed to help you find out the size of the market and the competition you face.

A window cleaning start-up illustrates how a hunch can prove to be a disaster, and then I will recommend some simple do-it-yourself research. A 50 year old marketing executive was made redundant with a six figure payoff. He lived in an up-market area and decided to launch a window cleaning service with uniformed cleaners, liveried vans, an expensive website and a direct mail campaign. As he would not be doing any window cleaning himself, he calculated that three cleaners would be needed from day one to provide him with sufficient income. He persevered for twelve months before admitting failure at a cost of nearly one hundred thousand.

Do-it-yourself research which should have been done includes:

Checking yellow pages to find out local window cleaners and telephoning them to find out:

- how long they have been in business
- how many cleaners they employ
- what areas they serve

Knocking on, say, 100 relevant doorsteps locally to ask:

- Do you have a regular window cleaner, or would you like to have one?

- Are you happy with your present window cleaner?

- What would persuade you to change?

- May I ask how much you pay? Or would be prepared to pay?

In this way, you should be able to assess the size of the market interested in having a window cleaner and, equally importantly, how willing or resistant people are to change to a different cleaner. The real-life situation failed because the local market was extensively covered and people saw no reason to change.

Write a convincing business plan to raise finance

Bank managers are reluctant to give a business overdraft or loan facility for a start-up on the basis of a meeting. Their procedures probably require a written business plan and, even if not, a plan will measurably increase your chance of raising the finance.

Before making an appointment to meet a bank manager, obtain a copy of their free guide to both starting a business and writing a business plan. These enable you to demonstrate that you know what is involved in a start-up and to present your business plan in the format they recommend.

Your concise business plan should outline:

- the name of the business
- the product or service, and approach to pricing
- the target market
- sales and marketing techniques
- a simple profit and loss account and cash flow.

Ideally your profit and loss account and cash flow should be presented monthly for the first year, and in outline for the next two years.

Recognize that if your plan shows a peak financing need of, say, £1,900 and you request a facility of £2,000, the bank manager will know you are likely to exceed the limit. Unexpected expenditure, slower than expected sales and late payment by customers should be expected and an adequate contingency allowed.

CASH FLOW IS TRULY A MATTER OF LIFE OR DEATH FOR EVERY BUSINESS

Cash flow is life or death

Making a profit is important, but cash flow is truly a matter of life or death for every business. Many people simply do not realize that even though a business has become profitable it can fail because cash has run out and additional finance cannot be raised.

Restaurants have one of the highest failure rates of any type of business. A typical scenario is that the chef-cum-owner lavishes expenditure on a state of the art kitchen, when the existing one was adequate, and trade does not build up sufficiently quickly to avoid failure because cash runs out.

Boring though it may seem, every business should have an annual cash flow plan, month-by-month, and monitor each month's actual cash flow compared to plan so that any danger signals are recognized promptly and corrective action is taken quickly.

Become a franchisee

Buying a franchise is a possible way to use a proven formula for success to fast-track you into your own business. Franchising is undoubtedly big business and there are hundreds of opportunities ranging from major brand names requiring a six figure investment, to part-time opportunities costing a few thousand.

Your starting point should be to get a free guide to franchising from a major bank or accountancy firm and to visit the website of franchising associations. Franchising 'fairs' are held in various locations for franchisers to showcase their offerings.

You should ideally select a business sector where you have relevant experience and an affinity with the produce or service.

Your investigation into a possible franchisee opportunity needs to include:

- When was the company founded and when was their franchising operation started?
- How many company owned and franchised outlets do they have? And what is their profit record?
- Obtain a set of company accounts to make sure it is financially stable
- How many franchises have failed or closed?

- Is the product or service likely to be long lived?

- How strongly branded is the business?

- Is the gross profit margin sufficiently attractive?

- Are the purchase cost and continuing royalty payments justified, compared with doing your own start-up?

Most important of all, however, is to talk face-to-face with two or three franchisees and to get feedback from a bank or accountancy firm which has a specialist franchise team.

Buy an established business

Buying any business is pregnant with risk! So much so, that it should be regarded as the opportunity of last resort. If you are really determined that this is the route you wish to take, I will outline essential steps you need to take to protect yourself:

- Do not believe the reason for sale given by the owners. In my experience, the real reason is often left unsaid and you need to find it out.

- Pay an accountant to check the validity of the profit and loss account for the past three years and the current year to date. You should take little comfort from the fact that the figures have been audited, because in a small business most of the input is provided by the owners.

- Investigate any vulnerability to retail premises; such as planning permission has been granted for a by-pass road or rumour that a supermarket or departmental store is to be built nearby.

- Ask searching questions of the owners such as:
    - Have you lost any significant customers recently?
    - Are you involved in any tax investigation, commercial dispute, litigation or unfair dismissal claim?
    - Do you comply with all regulatory controls and approvals?
- Pay an experienced lawyer to act for you to negotiate the purchase contract you will sign and to ensure you have adequate warranty protection and taxation liability indemnity.

Recognize that when a business changes ownership it often triggers some customers to buy elsewhere, so make an allowance in your future projections.

Above all, however, remember that comprehensive and rigorous investigation is essential before you buy.

Decide when to cash in your chips

Selling your business is an opportunity to realize serious wealth, and timing is important. If you sell too early, you will fail to capitalize on the full potential you could realize. Perhaps worse still, however, holding on too long may result in your business failing. Owners of consistently successful businesses naively assume things can only get better. Business success tends to come in cycles, and many small businesses are unable to adapt and prosper in the

NEVER RULE OUT SELLING A SUCCESSFUL BUSINESS, CREATING FINANCIAL SECURITY FOR YOU AND YOUR FAMILY, AND THEN STARTING ANOTHER BUSINESS IN DUE COURSE

face of technological change or new forms of competition. For example, retail travel agents have been hit hard by low cost airlines undermining demand for inclusive package holidays; the impact of cheaper products available on the internet; and airlines drastically reducing the amount of commission paid to intermediaries.

Add to the above, regulatory change, staff leaving to set up in competition to your business, the risk of ill health and the future becomes uncertain. So never rule out selling a successful business, creating financial security for you and your family, and then starting another business in due course.

Key point summary

1   recognize that self-employment or starting your own business is the key to becoming seriously richer and happier for most people

2   realize that self-employment and business start-up opportunities are all around you

3   prove your idea in your spare time to avoid the risk of giving up your job prematurely

4   passion, resilience, flexibility and competitiveness are essential personal traits for success

5   develop your sales and marketing skills from the outset

6   research your market and your competitors

7   write a convincing business plan to get your financing

8   prepare a month-by-month cash flow plan because cash flow determines success or failure

9   investigate thoroughly before buying a franchise or existing business.

TYPICAL CAPITAL GAINS FOR THE
MANAGEMENT TEAM RANGE FROM

20 TO 80 TIMES

THEIR ORIGINAL INVESTMENT AS A
RESULT OF A SUCCESSFUL EXIT

7 Pursue a management buy-out (MBO) or buy-in (MBI)

AN **MBO** OR **MBI** OFFERS senior executives a real opportunity to become a multi-millionaire within five years. Whilst the majority of deals exit successfully it will come as no surprise that some result in failure, and the executives lose their jobs and their investment. It is true to say, however, that the potential rewards dwarf the risk involved.

In the UK, the remainder of Europe and the USA there is a cash mountain available to fund MBO's and MBI's. Hundreds of deals are completed each year in the UK alone, and there is a shortage of quality management teams for the private equity houses to finance.

The essential ingredients for a successful MBO or MBI include:

1 a committed top management team
2 a suitable business
3 a carefully handled request to pursue a deal
4 an experienced corporate finance adviser
5 a convincing business plan
6 a compatible private equity house

7   a realistic timetable

8   expert legal and tax advice

9   satisfactory due diligence

10   awareness of the professional fees involved

11   addressing the requirements particular to MBI's.

Each of these will be considered separately.

A committed top management team

It must be recognized that the reality is a private equity house invests on the strength of the management team, first and foremost. Even if the business and the market sector are attractive, a private equity house will not invest unless they believe in the commitment and ability of the management team.

Private equity houses strongly prefer to back a management team led by an experienced managing director, and in the case of a group subsidiary company this should not present a problem. Private companies probably have the title of managing director occupied by one of the owners, but it is possible that the leader of the team already has profit responsibility as a divisional general manager. If not, then the case will have to be presented that the MBO leader had substantial de facto profit responsibility without the appropriate job title.

THE TYPICAL INVESTMENT REQUIRED FROM EACH MEMBER OF THE BUY-OUT TEAM IS ABOUT SIX MONTH'S SALARY

The next step is to establish there is a top management team committed to pursuing an MBO, typically no more than three or four people, and including a finance person. If one person does not wish to invest in the MBO, then it is still possible to proceed but with a stated commitment to replace them with someone prepared to invest, with recruitment commencing during the MBO process, so that an appointment can be made on legal completion or soon afterwards. If there is no suitable managing director to lead the team it is much more of a problem because it is difficult for the team to find their own leader.

The typical investment required from each member of the buy-out team is about six month's salary. The managing director is often invited to invest a third to a half more than other team members in order to benefit from a bigger equity stake. People may need to take a second mortgage on their home to finance their investment, but the potential capital gain makes it worthwhile. Most management buy-outs result in an exit by a trade sale or stockmarket listing within three to five years, and typical capital gains for the management team range from 20 to 80 times their original investment as a result of a successful exit.

A suitable business

Most private equity houses invest in businesses which cost from a few million to billions. Regional funds and business angels often invest in small businesses, so size is not necessarily an issue.

A loss-making business is not necessarily unsuitable, but the management team will need to outline a deliverable plan to restore profitability and cash generation quickly. This could involve closing loss making parts of the business, or eliminating group management charges or significant cost reduction. Generally speaking, identifiable 'cost out' opportunities are more convincing to private equity houses as a means of eliminating losses rather than sales growth which is likely to take longer to achieve.

The most important requirement for an MBO or MBI is positive cash generation within the first year or two. As MBO's and MBI's are financed by a substantial proportion of debt, it is important to reduce the interest burden as soon as possible by generating cash to repay some of the debt. Consequently, a cash hungry business may well be unsuitable such as a high technology company requiring subsequent injections of cash for research and development.

Tangible assets backing, primarily land and buildings, is helpful because it offers security for the debt finance, but it is not a prerequisite. A service company with low net asset backing, but with good growth and cash generation potential, will be seen as an attractive investment opportunity.

As the private equity house will probably be committed to an exit within five years, they need to be convinced that the business will still have demonstrable future prospects. Also, they will assess the most likely exit route and other possible avenues, including a secondary buy-out to other private equity houses, before they invest.

Interestingly, mature business sectors are quite attractive to private equity houses because the relatively low growth may make them attractive cash cows. Equally, some investors are attracted by a sector which is suffering a downturn because bargain prices may be available and by the time of exit the sector could well be enjoying better times.

Particular dependence on a single customer or product, or vulnerability to technological development or changing legislation will be viewed negatively by private equity investors. They are aware that MBO's and MBI's are usually paid for in full at legal completion, because it is not appropriate to give an earn-out deal to the vendors, although a trade buyer would do one to make the purchase price partly dependent on future performance.

A carefully handled request for an MBO

A request to pursue a management buy-out needs handling carefully, especially if the business is underperforming. The group or private owners may mistakenly think that the management team have allowed the business to underperform in order to reduce the purchase price. In some cases a request to pursue an MBO has lead to a swift dismissal of the team leader, so care really is needed. One way to minimize the risk is to meet a corporate finance boutique or an accountancy firm and, without appointing them at this stage or incurring any costs, get them to:

- assess the feasibility of finding financial backing for an MBO

- telephone the group or private owners, 'on behalf of a client', to find out if there is any prospect of considering an offer to buy the business. If not, the management team need to shelve the idea for the foreseeable future, but otherwise they can make a tactful approach with some confidence.

If a management team were to approach a private equity house and to disclose financial information about the business, without the express permission of the owners, there are grounds for and a real risk of summary dismissal. Consequently, private equity houses are reluctant to involve themselves with management teams in these circumstances because they are at risk of litigation for soliciting a purchase without permission.

Appoint an experienced corporate finance adviser

Every management team really does need a corporate finance advisor to pursue an MBO because of the complexity and amount of work involved. It would be quite wrong for the team to think that their previous experience of making acquisitions is sufficient to handle an MBO. It is NOT!

The role of the corporate finance adviser should include:

- assessing the suitability of the business and the experience of the management team for an MBO
- making the initial 'anonymous' approach to the group or owners to find out if they are prepared to consider a sale of the business
- guiding the management team to write a business plan and critiquing their draft
- picking three relevant private equity houses and telephoning a director to sell the deal
- sending the business plan to investors who are keen to meet the management team
- coaching the management team to handle the first meeting with private equity houses, because this may make or break the prospect of a deal
- negotiating a cost indemnity from the vendors, if possible, and ensuring that the management team do not have to pay any fees if a deal is not completed

- obtaining a period of exclusivity from the vendors, if possible, to pursue a deal without competing buyers

- negotiating the purchase of the business from the vendors

- negotiating the best possible equity deal for the management team from the private equity house

- helping the management team to select and beauty parade relevant lawyers and tax advisers, and to get their agreement to work on a contingent fee basis

- steering the deal safely to legal completion and handling any eleventh hour negotiations which often occur

- giving candid and objective advice to the management team throughout, and particularly recommending the deal should be aborted if unacceptable issues arise.

Three relevant corporate financial advisers should be interviewed before appointing one and asked the following questions:

- How many buy-outs has the firm, and most importantly the person you meet, completed of a similar size and complexity?

- Will the senior person you meet lead the transaction demonstrably from the front throughout?

- How many of their buy-outs have failed and why?

- Which private equity houses have invested in buy-outs they have advised upon? (To make sure they do not favour particular houses to win reciprocal business for themselves.)

- What will you do to ensure we obtain the maximum equity stake for our investment?

- Will you negotiate the purchase of the business for us from the owners?

- May we have the names and telephone numbers of three people for whom you have advised on their buy-out? (There is no substitute for telephone references on the individual advisers.)

- Are you prepared to invest some or all of your fee in the buy-out on the same terms as the private equity house? (A real test of their commitment.)

Write a convincing business plan

The management team must recognize that although they may have written lots of business plans, a different approach is required for presentation to prospective investors.

The business plan needs to convince the investor that the proposed buy-out is an attractive investment. It is primarily a selling document and should demonstrate the management team's commitment to the buy-out and the subsequent development of the business.

The business plan should be written by the management team. Their financial advisor should provide a critical and constructive review of the plan and the financial projections. The plan should ideally be no more than 15 to 25 pages long, plus appendices.

A typical business plan should include:

- an executive summary, preferably no longer than one page, covering the main points and setting out the situation with the vendors and the amount of finance required;

- a concise history of the business and a description of the products or services, markets served, distribution channels, location and size;

- an analysis of the market and the competitive position of the business;

- a description of the main assets and any key features of the way the business operates;

- a profile of the management team, their positions and responsibilities, their qualifications and experience, plus an overview of the staff; and

- summary results over the last two or three years and projections for the next three years showing profit and loss, cash flow and balance sheets.

The projections should be positive, credible and specific. Where the projections show rapid growth or a change in the nature of operations, the background and reasoning will need to be clearly spelt out.

An indication of likely acquisition costs should be included if known, together with any further funding requirements. It is generally not appropriate to outline funding structure.

Select a compatible private equity house or investor

Compatibility, personal chemistry and approach are vitally important. It is not enough to pick a private equity house or other investor, such as a business angel, on the financial aspects of the deal alone. Although a private equity house may not be the majority shareholder, they will insist on a shareholders agreement which gives them considerable control, especially if the business underperforms.

Although there are scores of private equity houses, each one invests in a given deal size range and may only invest in certain sectors or simply dislike some sectors. So this will reduce the number of prospective investors your corporate finance adviser can select from.

The approach of private equity houses differs in various ways because some:

- have a policy that the executive handling their investment will automatically become a non-executive director, so the initial contact should be with a compatible person

- search to find an appropriate external non-executive director and will listen to a suitable nomination from the management team

- have a reputation, possibly undeserved, for chiselling the deal for the management team at a late stage

- are hands-off

- become very much hands-on when a business underperforms and may seek changes to the management team

- are keen to achieve an early exit because investments in the particular fund must be realized by a closing date

- are keen to provide further funds to finance acquisitions, known as a 'buy and build' strategy, whilst others would resist.

You need to avoid ending up with a non-executive director whom you find arrogant, unsupportive or you simply dislike. So choose the private equity house and individual director whom you first meet accordingly.

Set a realistic timetable

Occasionally, a buy-out is legally completed within three months but most deals require five or six months.

A typical timetable of events is:

MONTH 1

- agree on the management team
- appoint financial advisers
- obtain agreement to pursue a management buy-out

MONTH 2

- write the business plan and send it to equity investors
- hold initial meetings with prospective equity investors
- seek a cost indemnity and period of exclusivity from the vendors

MONTH 3

- obtain outline written offers from prospective equity investors
- negotiate improved terms with equity investors
- appoint preferred equity investor and your lawyers

MONTH 4

- negotiate the acquisition from the vendors
- sign heads of agreement
- investigating accountants complete due diligence

MONTHS 5/6

- equity investor syndicates equity if appropriate
- arrange debt finance
- prepare and negotiate legal documents
- renegotiate the equity deal for management, if necessary
- legally complete the management buy-out as soon as possible.

Appoint expert lawyers and tax advisers

The legal work is more complex in a buy-out than in a similar acquisition by a trade buyer, so it is essential that your lawyers have relevant experience. The private equity house will appoint lawyers on behalf of 'Newco', the investment vehicle, to buy the company and to handle their contract with the management team. The debt provider will appoint their own advisers. The management team must have their own lawyers to negotiate their contract with the private equity house. Issues of real importance to the management team that need to be negotiated include:

- service contracts, and especially the conditions imposed on an executive who leaves before the exit is achieved

- the freedom for management to make capital expenditure decisions, recruit senior staff and award salary increases to staff

- the warranties and indemnities to be undertaken by the management team.

Expert advice is needed before the management buy-out is legally completed in order to ensure the maximum benefit for the management team after paying income and capital gains tax.

Issues that need to be addressed are:

- the availability of income tax relief on the interest paid on borrowings to purchase an equity stake;

- legitimate opportunities to minimize capital gains tax and inheritance tax liabilities in due course under current taxation regulations; and

- income tax relief on the purchase price of the equity stake should the business fail after the management buy-out.

Satisfactory due diligence

Any investor will require comprehensive due diligence, otherwise they have every right not to invest or to renegotiate the price and conditions of the deal. The fact that the management team know the business intimately is simply not good enough.

In addition to commercial, financial, tax and legal due diligence, the management team should expect their own personal history and business track record to be checked. Also, equity investors and debt providers will be particularly sensitive to any environmental issues that may arise.

Their concern will extend beyond the business having all the necessary approvals, permits and licences necessary to operate and will include the state of the fabric of any buildings and of any surrounding property. Funders will wish to establish any manner in which any property assets, over which security may be granted, may be affected by environmental issues as well as any liabilities which might be incurred by Newco or indeed, the funders themselves.

Environmental legislation can make both occupiers, owners and 'polluters' liable for environmental problems. As a minimum, most funders will insist on a 'Phase One' environmental investigation of a business with manufacturing or property assets.

Professional fees involved

Newco pays all professional fees on legal completion, which are treated as the cost of acquiring the company. The corporate finance advisers must ensure that the management team are not responsible for any unexpected fees if the buy-out does not complete for any reason. This means that the professional advisers acting for the management team must all accept a wholly or predominantly contingent fee basis.

Management teams are often shocked by the long list of fees to be paid, and the total bill, which includes:

1 corporate finance advice

2 an arrangement fee of the amount provided, often between one and two percent depending upon the size of the deal, for both the private equity house and the debt provider

3 legal fees for the management team, the equity investor and the debt provider

4 tax advice

5 any pension advice required

6 due diligence

The total fees for a smaller buy-out are likely to reach nearly 10% of the purchase price, and will rarely be less than 4% for a large deal. An important factor which increases fees to these levels is that most of the people involved are working on a contingent fee basis, and it can never be assumed that a buy-out is certain to be legally completed.

THE TOTAL FEES FOR A SMALLER BUY-OUT ARE LIKELY TO REACH NEARLY 10% OF THE PURCHASE PRICE

Particular requirements of MBI's

If there is no opportunity for you to achieve an MBO of the business you work in, an MBI may provide you with the chance to achieve comparable wealth.

Equity investors recognize that there is a greater risk inherent in an MBI compared to an MBO, because a buy-out team should have intimate and up-to-date knowledge of the business. Consequently, private equity houses look for a chief executive with relevant sector experience. They are not persuaded by the argument that a chief executive can be effective in any business.

Time is the real enemy of every MBI candidate. It is difficult to find sufficient time to search for a suitable company available to buy whilst employed in a demanding full-time job, and when the time comes to pursue a deal in earnest you will probably have to give up your job and income.

You need to be realistic about the total time required. Research shows that a typical MBI requires almost 18 months from starting the search to legal completion, and completing the deal will take up to six months of the total time involved. So before giving up a highly paid job, make sure you have enough cash available to finance the time you need without an income and still have sufficient money available to invest.

CONCENTRATE ON IDENTIFYING TARGET COMPANIES WHERE YOUR EXPERIENCE MAKES YOU THE IDEAL CANDIDATE

A suitable target company available to acquire is the key to achieving an MBI. Some private equity houses maintain MBI candidate registers, primarily for chief executives and finance directors, and may organize networking events. Some recruitment firms serve only the private equity community and so it makes sense for you to register with them.

Unfortunately, this is no guarantee of success because there us a surfeit of MBI candidates. Some companies exist to pay a salary to suitable MBI candidates to help them search for an investment opportunity which they will finance, and a few corporate finance boutiques will provide research facilities and office support to help outstanding MBI candidates to find an opportunity. Clearly, these avenues improve your chances measurably but do not guarantee success.

It must be recognized, however, that both corporate vendors and business owners will be sceptical of your ability to finance the deal. You can improve your creditability by meeting a private equity house and persuading them to write to you outlining their willingness to finance you in a given sector up to a stated purchase price. Alternatively, you could ask an accountancy firm or a corporate finance boutique to make the approach on your behalf without revealing it is a potential MBI.

Focus is the key to a successful search for an MBI opportunity. Focus on the type of company which your track record makes you the ideal candidate to be chief executive. A company you have previously worked for is particularly relevant because you have already been selected for the job before now.

If a previous company has to be ruled out, concentrate on identifying target companies where your experience makes you the ideal candidate. Relevant experience is a crucial factor for a private equity house to back an MBI. You must realize that private equity houses, corporate finance advisers and MBI job registers are literally swamped by candidates who set their target company search criteria so wide that thousands of companies would fit the bill. These people are written off as hopeless wannabes.

Focus will make you a much more attractive candidate. Your search criteria may be as narrow as:

- a company in the corporate event management sector
- with a turnover of between £10 and £30 million
- which will be developed to become a market leader in key business sectors within the corporate event industry
- located in the south.

What is more, you were previously managing director of a similar company and you live in the south, so credibility is firmly established.

Key point summary

1 recognize that investors are backing the management team, and especially the chief executive, first and foremost

2 the ability to generate a positive cash flow is the most important attribute of a business for an MBO

3 realize that an ill-judged request for an MBO could result in your dismissal

4 appoint an experienced corporate finance adviser at the outset

5 recognize that first impressions really do count, so your initial meeting with investors is make or break

6 write a convincing business plan, because 70% of plans are rejected without even meeting the management team

7 personal chemistry, compatibility and the approach of your investor are important

8 expert legal and tax advice are essential

9 the key to an MBI is to find the investment opportunity yourself, and focus is the key to your success.

Part Two

Become truly happier as well

A COMBINATION OF SENSIBLE LIVING, MODERATION AND BALANCE IS LIKELY TO PAY HUGE DIVIDENDS

EXERCISE ABOUNDS IN GOOD INTENTIONS, AND MANY PEOPLE QUICKLY FALL BY THE WAYSIDE

8

Manage your health

IT WOULD BE RECKLESS TO single-mindedly pursue wealth and not pay ample attention to your health. The consequences may well be dire. A mental breakdown or addiction can happen in your twenties just as easily as later in life. Your earning power, ability to create wealth and your happiness may be wrecked.

A combination of sensible living, moderation and balance is likely to pay huge dividends. Appropriate habits and routines are easily developed. The aspects of your health which require positive action include:

1 weight
2 diet
3 exercise
4 sleep
5 stress management
6 relaxation techniques
7 work-free periods
8 leisure and holidays

9   alcohol

10 smoking

11 drugs

12 gambling

13 positive mental attitudes

14 invest money in your health

15 a personal action plan.

Each of these will be considered separately.

Weight

Your weight is important for good health at any age. The view that you will not be at risk until you are middle aged is incorrect. The reality is that as the years pass it will become harder to lose weight and less likely that you will.

Excess weight may work against you in other ways. Some employers are prejudiced against excess weight, perhaps wrongly assuming that it is a sign of laziness or that it does not fit the 'corporate image'. Unfair, but it could adversely affect your getting the job you want. Equally, excess weight may work against you attracting the partner you want.

Check your weight using the following Body Mass Index.

Your BODY MASS INDEX (BMI) gives an indication of your weight in relation to your height. It's a general guide only – acceptable levels are determined by your sex, build, or amount of muscle. See your doctor if you're worried that your weight may be affecting your health.

Body Mass Index

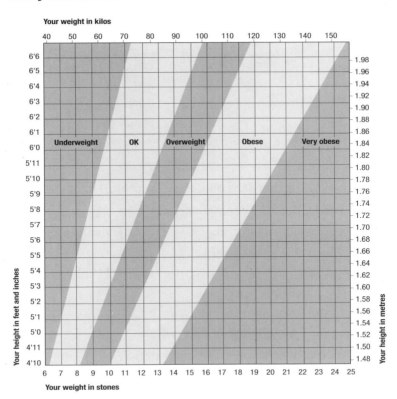

YOU SHOULD EAT PLENTY OF FRUIT AND VEGETABLES EVERY DAY

Before deciding to lose weight, which will require a change in your diet and/or start taking more exercise, you are strongly advised to visit your doctor. The evidence is overwhelming that sudden weight loss is likely to be temporary and can damage your health, so reject any notion of pursuing a crash diet. Your best chance of lasting weight loss is to gradually lose weight, perhaps as little as half a kilogram per week, over a reasonable period during which time you have developed healthier eating habits and are taking more exercise.

Diet

Eating the same foods, but in smaller quantities, inevitably means that when you stop 'dieting' the weight is likely to return. The aim should be to change your diet, and this does not necessarily mean that you are continually feeling hungry.

Foods to avoid or to regard only as an occasional treat include:

- fried foods
- fatty foods
- chocolates
- sweets
- potato crisps
- cakes
- cream
- thick sauces
- biscuits
- soft drinks.

If this sounds draconian, do not despair. Even some compromizes are better than doing nothing, for example:

- choose lean bacon rather than streaky
- grill bacon rather than fry it, and place it on a paper towel to absorb any surface fat

- use low fat oven ready chips rather than deep frying
- use low fat cream instead of full cream
- choose low fat products such as biscuits and crisps, but recognize the sugar or fat content is still likely to be quite high
- scramble eggs rather than fry them.

Foods to eat in moderation include:

- red meat
- eggs
- processed foods
- cheese
- salad cream
- offal
- butter
- coffee.

Processed foods include tinned and frozen products which may contain surprisingly high quantities of sugar, salt or fat.

Foods which are good for you include:

- salads
- fruit
- vegetables, including potatoes
- fish, especially oily fish such as salmon and mackerel
- pasta, but avoid thick, creamy sauces
- bread
- cereals
- beans
- lentils
- white meat.

Potatoes should be boiled or baked, not sautéd or roasted. Ideally, meat and fish should be grilled. Bread should be brown or wholemeal rather than white. Olive oil is healthier than processed salad dressings. Basically you should eat plenty of fruit and vegetables every day as they are unlikely to increase your weight.

THE KEY TO EXERCISE IS THAT IT SHOULD BE REGULAR, ENJOYABLE AND RESULT IN BREAKING INTO A SWEAT BUT NOT FINISHING EXHAUSTED

Monitoring your weight loss needs an accurate set of bathroom scales, but only check your weight once a week as to do it daily in unrealistic and unduly anxious.

Exercise

It really is important to visit your doctor before embarking on an exercise programme. Plunging headlong into vigorous exercise can be harmful to your health, and may result in painful pulled muscles and suchlike.

Exercise abounds in good intentions, and many people quickly fall by the wayside. Even joining a gym club may result in an initial burst of regular exercise which soon wanes. The key to exercise is that it should be regular, enjoyable and result in breaking into a sweat but not finishing exhausted. Getting into the habit of regular exercise is important, such as:

- Every morning before you shower, do an aerobic exercise routine or spend time on an exercise cycle, a rowing machine or a treadmill. You can even take the opportunity to watch the morning news on television whilst you are exercising.

- Every morning when the weather is dry, get off the train or bus a kilometre or two before your usual stop and walk to work

- Similarly, use your lunch break to take a brisk walk.

- Always walk briskly up and down the stairs at work instead of using lifts. Better still, occasionally walk up and down several floors purely for exercise.

SLEEP REPAIRS BOTH THE BODY AND THE MIND

- When choosing a gym club pick one close to your office so that you can visit before work, because there are always built in excuses and distractions at lunchtime or at the end of the day.

- If your gym club is close to home, and doesn't open before you leave for work, make a point of visiting on your way home, because once you get home then it requires a greater effort to go out again to the gym.

- Provided your general fitness is good enough, jog or cycle to and from work regularly.

- Choose a game you enjoyed playing at school and join a team which plays primarily for exercise and enjoyment such as five-a-side soccer or hockey or cricket.

- Join with friends in a regular social game of tennis or squash.

Sleep

Adequate sleep is important for good health. Sleep repairs both the body and the mind. The immediate effect of inadequate sleep is not only tiredness, but reduced work effectiveness, poor concentration and the increased risk of accidents, especially when driving. The effect of continued lack of sleep is to risk undermining your health and to make you more vulnerable to infection and illness.

A pragmatic test of sufficient sleep is that you should wake up feeling physically and mentally refreshed. The amount of sleep people need varies, and often reduces with older age, but many adults need at least seven hours sleep a night. In a way, you have a bank account for sleep. When a late night means that you have too little sleep, top up your sleep account by having a brief sleep during the next day or ensuring you have ample sleep the following night.

Some executives are prone to macho displays of coping with sleep deprivation after an overnight long haul flight by working through the following day. Mental powers and concentration are significantly diminished, and worse still, the effects of jet lag may last for several days. It is much better to take a bath or shower, and benefit from a relaxed day spending time in sunlight, or at least enjoying fresh air, and doing some gentle physical exercise, all of which will minimize the effect and duration of jet lag.

Many people sleep much sounder and longer on holiday than when working, for the simple reason that the combination of more fresh air, exercise and a relaxed mind are powerful and natural sedatives. The inability to get to sleep quickly and easily or waking up early already thinking about work or personal problems cannot be allowed to continue. If increased fresh air and exercise, together with deliberate mental relaxation before trying to sleep do not cure the problem, medical advice is required. Sleeping pills should be regarded as only a temporary solution, because they can quickly become addictive or at least a necessary crutch and often leave people feeling jaded for a period after waking up.

Stress management

Stress comes from within, caused by external circumstances and pressures. Whilst acceptable levels of stress are quite healthy and normal, undue stress is harmful and potentially seriously damaging. Stress is a major issue in the workplace, and increasingly employers are addressing it constructively.

Stress is indiscriminate, and can affect literally everyone from the chief executive to a recently joined college leaver.

When stress begins to reach unacceptable levels at work, the most sensible course of action is to raise the matter with your immediate manager. All too often, people suffer in silence when the problem is easily overcome by more equitable work sharing, some additional training or, if necessary, arranging a job transfer internally.

For someone suffering stress, symptoms which require urgent medical help include:

- working excessive amounts of overtime and, not surprisingly, failing to cope any better with the problems or workload
- increasingly 'shuffling work around', rather than tackling it effectively, and falling further behind
- an inability to concentrate and focus on work effectively
- a tendency towards rambling and incoherent conversation

- an inability to switch off mentally

- problems getting to sleep and/or waking up early already in a mental turmoil

- an increasing consumption of alcohol or drugs.

If you recognize any of the previous symptoms in yourself, do not procrastinate but do visit your doctor without delay.

Relaxation techniques

Some people find they benefit enormously from regularly using relaxation techniques, while others dismiss them as pure bunkum. At the simplest level, breathing and gentle stretching exercises can be helpful to people who are stressed or physically wound up. On the other hand, ancient techniques such as yoga and tai chi are based upon established techniques and proven principles.

OUR GOAL SHOULD BE THAT AS A ROUTINE YOU DO NOT VISIT THE OFFICE AT THE WEEKEND

If you have difficulties relaxing, then the familiar message is to find out more by visiting websites, reading books and magazine articles. Alternatively, there are yoga and other specialist classes widely available, or individual training by a personal coach.

Create work-free periods

It is not enough to be able to switch off from work, the rule should be to create regular work free periods when you do switch off completely. If you are unable to organize your working life so that every weekend there is one day when you simply forget about work, something is wrong. It suggests a marked workaholic trait. Your goal should be that as a routine you do not visit the office at the weekend, the only exception would be when there is a particular deadline to be achieved or a one-off task to be completed urgently.

Mobile 'phones are intrusive. If you find that you are receiving incoming calls regularly on Saturdays and Sundays, there is a simple remedy. Switch your work mobile 'phone onto voicemail, and buy another mobile for personal calls.

Leisure and holidays

Your non-working time should be at least as enjoyable and fulfilling as work. It is barren and boring simply to take time off from work and to do very little. Those people who either boast or admit that they wouldn't know how to fill their time on retirement, need to start remedying the problem right away. Decades ago, retirement happened predictably between the ages of 60 and 65. Nowadays, enforced retirement can happen when people are in their 40s and 50s, because they simply may not be able to get another job which they are prepared to accept.

Leisure time should be enjoyable, active, social and varied.

HOLIDAYS ARE AN ESSENTIAL PART OF PERSONAL HEALTH MANAGEMENT

Active is not meant to suggest undue physical exercise, but does reject spending long periods watching television or casually surfing the internet. Social means spending time with family and friends, and enjoying the company of other people by playing sport, a shared hobby or special interest groups. If your work is achievement orientated and competitive, leisure activities may well play down competitive pastimes.

Holidays are an essential part of personal health management. Your full holiday entitlement should be planned and taken. Spending holidays at home, doing very little, may save money but it is a waste. Regard the cost of holidays as an investment. If you find it takes several days to wind down on holiday, that is a clear signal you are leading an unduly stressful life. Take two or three weeks continuous holiday so that you do manage to switch off and relax.

A holiday should provide a complete break from work and a change of routine. Whether it is a beach holiday or strenuous mountain climbing, you should return physically and mentally rejuvenated.

Alcohol

Alcohol is enjoyable, furthermore current medical evidence is that it is probably healthier to have a glass or two of wine a day, particularly red, than to be teetotal. Moderation is crucial, even if it is boring. Alcohol addiction creeps up on people. The recommended guidelines of not more than 21 units a week for men (a unit is a medium-sized glass of wine or half a pint of lager), and 14 units a week for women should not be exceeded.

Possible signs of alcohol addiction include:

- thinking about your first drink of the day almost from the time you awake
- finding an excuse to take your first drink even before bars and public houses open, perhaps by adding a shot of whisky to your coffee
- drinking when you are alone in the house
- secret drinking when family members tell you that you are drinking excessively
- a tendency to keep on drinking until the bottle is empty
- violence and abusiveness caused by drink
- rewarding yourself with a drink whenever things are not going well
- having a stiff drink before going out in order 'to get in the mood'.

MODERATION IS CRUCIAL, EVEN IF IT IS BORING

Alcoholism causes some people to lose their career, their partner, their children and their home, in a process which can be thoroughly degrading. Alcoholism is for life. Very few alcoholics, if any, succeed in being able to drink in a controlled way once they have overcome their excessive drinking. One alcoholic drink is often sufficient to trigger the problem again. So the message should be quite clear, if you are regularly exceeding the recommended limit or are showing signs of possible alcohol dependence, either reduce your drinking if you can, or immediately seek medical advice and help. Delay is potentially unthinkably dangerous.

A simple way to demonstrate that you are not dependent on alcohol is to have at least one alcohol free day a week or to occasionally have an alcohol free week or month. If it will help, persuade a friend to do the same and stiffen each other's resolve.

Smoking

Smoking cannot be justified or defended. Smoking causes many premature deaths and widespread illness. Cutting down consumption is not an option, because there is a strong likelihood any reduction will only be temporary. Waiting to make a New Year's resolution is unacceptable delay. Take action now. The first step should be to consult your doctor. Products such as nicotine patches have helped many thousands of people to stop smoking.

IF THE PRESSURE OF WORK CAUSES YOU TO TAKE DRUGS, CHANGE YOUR JOB

WAITING TO MAKE A NEW YEAR'S RESOLUTION IS UNACCEPTABLE DELAY. TAKE ACTION NOW

Drugs

Cannabis may be harmless and may not be addictive; but the evidence is far from conclusive and seemingly it is only a question of time before more countries will legalize the personal use of cannabis or at least de-criminalize it. On the other hand, some drugs are addictive or dangerous or both. The expressions '*social drugs*' and '*social drug taking*' are a complete misnomer. Ecstasy has killed people and cocaine is addictive. If the pressure of work causes you to take drugs, change your job. If drug taking is commonplace amongst your friends and you feel pressured to join them, change your friends. Drugs are a crutch which can and should be discarded now. Medical advice and help is available, substitute products are available to help overcome dependency, residential clinics provide help to deal with addiction.

Gambling

Occasional gambling is fun and not harmful. Millions buy lotto tickets every week and will never become remotely addicted to gambling. It is a fact, however, that gambling can become addictive and does wreck lives. One sign of a growing gambling problem is when someone is gambling and losing more that they can afford, even without some aspect of their life suffering. Your local doctor will provide advice and access to counselling or Gamblers Anonymous as appropriate. People with a gambling problem must be urged to seek professional help without delay.

Positive mental attitudes

Positive mental attitudes have a favourable impact on your life, and probably contribute to better health.

The most important one is self-esteem. High self-esteem is often accompanied by high achievement, fulfilment and happiness. Whilst a low self-esteem undermines achievement and content-ment because of self doubt.

In simple terms, self-esteem requires liking yourself. Everyone can find things about their body appearance, habits and personality they are unhappy about. As the popular songs say *'accentuate the positive and eliminate the negative'* is the approach to adopt. Rein-force your self-esteem by rehearsing your achievements and favourable attributes.

Other mental attitudes to develop include:

- being positive rather than negative, and optimistic rather than pessimistic

- smiling frequently and being cheerful rather than having a reputation for being grumpy

- having an inner self-belief and self-assurance rather than self-doubt

- displaying poise, especially under pressure, and never being guilty of uncontrolled outbursts

- being spontaneous, open and straightforward rather than guarded and introspective.

HIGH SELF-ESTEEM IS OFTEN ACCOMPANIED BY HIGH ACHIEVEMENT, FULFILMENT AND HAPPINESS

Consider investing money in your health

In addition to changing your lifestyle, as outlined earlier in this chapter, you should consider investing money in your health as well. Remember, without good health your wealth may count for little and your ability to earn or to create wealth may be undermined. So you should view the prospect of spending money to protect your health as cost effective insurance.

Unless your employer provides you with private medical insurance, seriously consider making your own arrangements. A key benefit of private medicine is the opportunity to visit a consultant or to have an operation quickly, which may well avoid further problems.

Health screening is available even if you do not have private medical insurance. Some doctors support regular screening because it may provide an early warning of a medical condition, whilst other doctors question the need and benefits. So it is a matter for your personal choice.

GAMBLING CAN BECOME ADDICTIVE AND DOES WRECK LIVES

State doctors operate under tough budgetary guidelines, and consequently may be reluctant to prescribe expensive drugs. If you sense or know this is happening to you, seriously consider arranging to see a private doctor who will recommend the most effective drugs for you, but you will have to pay for them.

Personal action plan

Good intentions are not enough, and neither is a key point summary to remind you of the key points. Positive action is needed, so use the following format to create a personal action plan and monitor your progress.

Health management action plan

Date _____ Weight _____

Diet _____
_____

Exercise _____
_____

Sleep _____
_____

Stress _____
_____

Relaxation techniques _____
_____

Work-free periods _____
_____

Leisure and holidays _____
_____

Alcohol, smoking, drugs and gambling _____
_____

Mental attitudes _____
_____

THE MOST COMMONLY QUOTED REASON GIVEN FOR FAILED SHOW-BUSINESS MARRIAGES IS THAT WORKING AND LIVING APART DESTROYED THE RELATIONSHIP

9 Invest time in family and friends

A RECURRING MESSAGE IN THIS book is that becoming richer and happier should go hand-in-hand. Investing time in family and friends will bring you much happiness, and it really is folly to think that you can single-mindedly pursue wealth first, and find time for family and friends later. By then it may be too late. You need to get your work life balance so that you always do have time for family and friends.

All of the following people need to feel special because you make them special by giving the gift of time:

- your partner or spouse
- your parents
- your children
- other relatives
- friends and acquaintances.

If you fail to invest the time required, you may well have to cope effectively with:

- separation and divorce
- bereavement and terminal illness
- finding a partner.

Also, develop the habit of giving gifts that really count. Each of these will be considered separately.

Your partner or spouse

The saying that absence makes the heart grow fonder must be distrusted. The most commonly quoted reason given for failed show-business marriages is that working and living apart destroyed the relationship. If you spend all hours at work, and do not have any children at home, your partner may be lonely. When there are children to be cared for, your partner may feel imprisoned. Either way it could lead to a breakdown in the relationship.

The solution is neither complex nor secret. Like many things in life it requires common sense, some effort and balance. Tangible action which enhances personal relationships with a partner includes:

- Make sure you remember birthdays, anniversaries and Valentine's Day. Cards need to be given at breakfast time, with a present which shows personal thought. A cheque, however generous, is unlikely to be as welcome as a thoughtfully chosen gift. If you are prone to forget, diarise the event to allow sufficient time to get a card and a gift.

- Celebrate birthdays and anniversaries on the actual date. When works gets in the way of the actual anniversary date, a celebration either before or after is likely to be viewed as second best.

- When you are going away overnight on business, leave a card behind with a thoughtful message as well as telephoning home during your trip. Whenever possible, but not necessarily every trip, buy a small gift.

- Surprise gifts, even if small, show you care.

- When arguments occur, as they inevitably do, avoid blame, insult and harsh words. The aim should be to understand your partner's point of view and the cause of dissatisfaction so that an agreeable way forward can be reached. Every attempt should be made to reach an amicable conclusion at the time. Sulking and not speaking are childish behaviour which cannot be excused. A good maxim is never to go to sleep without having resolved an argument.

- Bringing up past arguments or failings which have been put right is counterproductive and should be avoided. If an agreement to change a behaviour pattern does not achieve the desired change, however, then the subject should be raised again.

- Some couples spend a lot of time together and never really communicate. Effective communication in a partnership is not just about relating the events of the day to each other or discussing topical issues, important though these are. It is important to understand your partner's feelings and to be sensitive to any signals. When these occur, find out what is the cause. Better still, develop the habit of telling each other your anxieties, concerns and problems promptly.

SURPRISE GIFTS, EVEN IF SMALL, SHOW YOU CARE

- Make some time to talk to each other everyday, free from the distractions of the internet, newspapers, television or any other distraction.

- Make a top priority of being there when you are really needed such as providing comfort for important medical appointments.

Your parents

Parent can often be the forgotten relatives, especially when their adult children are juggling the priorities of work, home and a young family. Parents make sacrifices willingly for their children, and do not expect to be repaid later. The sad reality is, however, that some people only realize the situation when a parent dies prematurely or suddenly, and then wish they had taken the opportunity to treat their parents differently or to have seen more of them. Simple things to do include:

- Remembering birthdays and anniversaries for parents by a card and a gift is fine, but the gift of time is likely to be appreciated much more. Organize your life so that you can spend some time with them on their birthdays and anniversaries.

- Making landmark events, such as retirement, a special wedding anniversary or a 'major' birthday, a day to remember. A party or event will need organizing, but you are likely to find it equally rewarding.

- Inviting parents to spend part of Christmas with you, and especially for them to enjoy seeing their grandchildren opening presents.

- Arranging family holidays together, at least occasionally.

- Offering support when one parent dies, and recognizing that loneliness may become a major problem. Birthdays and anniversaries can bring back the sense of loss, so be available to provide company and support. If loneliness is a problem, be available to talk through the situation and ensure that positive action is taken.

Grandparents find visits from their grandchildren, and any great grandchildren, a source of joy and a special event to look forward to.

So make sure that you find time to visit them or to invite your grandparents to visit you.

Your children

Parenthood does not come with a manual designed to ensure success, because indeed some people feel that they have done 'all the right things' only to see their children go off the rails. In truth parenthood means simple and rather obvious things, and hoping for the best, including:

- Establishing basic ground rules as early as possible, without being disciplinarian, because children need to have behavioural guidelines.

- Teaching values and principles, which hopefully become second nature to them, by personal example. Remember that children often mirror their parents behaviour in adult life, for better or for worse, and this includes smoking, drinking, drug taking, dishonesty and violence.

- Providing the best possible education opportunities compatible with a child's abilities and aptitudes. To send a child to an overdemanding school creates undue pressure and may result in a poorer level of achievement. Equally, to encourage a teenager to choose a prestigious and overly academic university compared to their ability is misplaced and selfish. Most children will achieve more in an environment suited to their aptitudes, interests and level of academic ability.

MAKE TIME TO SPEND WITH YOUR CHILDREN AND TO PLAY WITH THEM

- Rationing the amount of time spent watching television and playing computer games, whilst encouraging children to play with other children and take physical exercise in the process.

- Recognizing that a major benefit of nursery school is to learn social skills by playing with other children and any academic learning should be regarded as secondary.

- Encouraging and developing social skills such as politeness, good manners, courtesy, unselfishness, generosity, sharing and correct eating habits.

- Making time to spend with your children and to play with them.

- Attending birthdays, school plays, sports days, prize giving (especially if your child has not won a prize) and parents' evenings. It is inexcusable to allow work to get in the way except for unusual circumstances. Make a point of diarizing every date as soon as you know it.

- Encouraging children to have an open mind and not to say they do not like something unless they have tried it and, equally importantly, not foisting your personal prejudices onto them.

Your other relatives

Family members can be a source of comfort and support in times of need. **Invest time** with siblings, cousins, aunts and uncles. Family get togethers do not have to be boring affairs. Take the initiative and organize an event which involves doing something together. Something as simple as a barbecue could be enjoyable. Similarly, hiring a boat for a river cruise should not be prohibitively expensive. All that is required is a little imagination.

Your friends and acquaintances

Making friends at work and spending time with colleagues socially can be enjoyable, but often much of this contact comes to an end or is sharply diminished on leaving or retirement. When colleagues socialize together conversation often centres around work or office gossip and usually is singularly boring and irritating for partners.

Friends and acquaintances should provide an escape from work.

Time and effort needs to be made to spend with existing friends and to make new ones. If you are mostly unavailable to accept invitations from friends, even for an informal drink, because work intervenes or you are otherwise committed, do not be surprised if eventually the invitations dry up.

Coping with separation and divorce

Divorce and separation are commonplace, but this does not make them any easier to handle. Divorce rates of about 40 per cent occur in many countries. In the UK the average length of a first marriage is only 10 years, and seven years for a second marriage.

Separation may just have happened to you, so the advice on your relationship with your partner contained earlier in this chapter may have come too late. Separation and divorce so often bring stress and unhappiness to both partners, and any children will suffer although it may not be apparent until considerably later. If the relationship was worthwhile and can possibly be restored, every effort should be made to do so. Counselling is widely available and has proved effective for many people. Sadly some people dismiss it out of hand, perhaps because they mistakenly think it is an admission of weakness.

Separation may be inevitable, however, and everyone should recognize that some people, men and women alike, are devastated by the experience. Furthermore, it is difficult to predict how well anyone will cope, because sometimes it is the most unlikely people who are devastated. Commonsense and practical guidelines for coping with separation and divorce include:

- Recognizing that even though one partner terminated the relationship, both people undoubtedly contributed to the situation.

- Acting coolly and calmly throughout, despite the temptation to retaliate and provoke.

- Quickly making separate accommodation arrangements to avoid the confrontation likely to ensue from prolonged personal contact.

- Getting advice from any relatives and friends who have separated or divorced, because people without similar experience may well be singularly ill equipped to understand how you feel and to recommend what you should consider doing.

- Making sure that the best interests of any children are taken care of. Criticism aimed at the other parent or subjecting children to any form of tug of war can only be harmful. Children need reassurance and stability more than ever.

- Finding a suitable solicitor and ideally one that will do everything possible to achieve an equitable settlement without any undue provocation whatsoever. Retaliation only produces retaliation and higher legal costs.

- Avoid putting mutual friends in the invidious position of having to choose one partner or the other to support. Some people are likely to take sides, and sadly this has to be accepted when it happens, but things don't have to be this way. It is perfectly possible to maintain a friendship with both partners, albeit separately.

- Maintaining a relationship with your former partner to enable both of you to attend family events together and to share children's birthdays, school sports days and parents' evenings without any risk of acrimony.

The fact remains, however, that some people are devastated, intensely lonely and unable to function properly at work.

An experienced doctor gave the following advice for coping in these circumstances:

- Live life only one day at a time, and stop worrying about the future. Time is a great healer and although it seems that things will never get better when in the depths of despair, they inevitably will in due course.

- Seek to fill every day in order to minimize loneliness and despair. If necessary, temporarily work all hours in order to keep mentally occupied.

- Realize that people do not want to spend time with people full of self pity, but will gladly help people who are making an effort to overcome the situation.

- Avoid crutches such as sleeping pills, unless temporary and under medical supervision, excessive amounts of alcohol and drugs, because all of these will never solve the problem and could lead to dependency.

This whole section on coping with separation and divorce may seem like an impossible counsel of perfection. This may be so, but in your heart you know it is sensible advice and, more importantly, it works.

TALKING ABOUT THE DEPARTED PERSON IS AN IMPORTANT PART IN COMING TO TERMS WITH DEATH

Coping with bereavement and terminal illness

Everyone faces the difficult prospect of coping with a family bereavement at some point in life, and many will encounter a family member enduring a terminal illness. When either of these happens, the feeling may be of temporary but absolute numbness of thought. Life has to go on, however, and this observation is not intended to be remotely callous or even insensitive.

The advice given earlier for coping with separation and divorce is equally applicable and effective. Bereavement counselling is widely available and has helped many people. Tears are understandable; grief needs an escape valve and no attempt should be made to hide it. Equally, talking about the departed person is an important part in coming to terms with death.

TIME IS ONE OF THE GREATEST GIFTS TO GIVE

Terminal illness may seem tantamount to a prolonged period of helplessness, but this attitude is far removed from what can and should happen. Time is one of the greatest gifts to give. Personal ambition and a career should be put on hold at the very least, and if necessary leave of absence or part-time working must be negotiated. If your employer is unwilling to accommodate your need, be prepared to resign. An obvious priority is to secure the best possible care and treatment, but comfort, support and listening are personal gifts to be given generously. Hospices are fulfilling and inspirational places, positively focussing on the quality of life, and should be pursued as a valuable opportunity.

Finding a partner

For some people finding a partner is of overwhelming importance. Yet frustratingly, it is one of the things in life when trying too hard can be counterproductive.

Fortunately, finding a partner can happen in the most unlikely circumstances and when one is not remotely even thinking about it. To someone keen to find a partner, however, this may be of little comfort. There are positive steps one can take to maximize the chances including:

- Making the most of your appearance.

- Pursuing group activities with like-minded people, and this is equally relevant at any age. Classes in conversational French or photography, the gym, tennis or hockey club are just a few of the countless opportunities to meet people which should be enjoyable in their own right.

- Displaying a positive mental outlook.

- Becoming a better conversationalist. Taking an interest in current issues helps, and so does being aware of and interested in a wide range of subjects. Conversation is a technique in its own right, however, and the internet and books will provide practical tips.

- Joining a dating agency or a social group for single people, or using the internet, but some people will emphatically reject these.

Gifts that count

This may seem a strange item to include in a chapter devoted to family and social relationships.

Generosity is an attractive quality, but thoughtfulness can often be much more valuable and appreciated than the monetary value of a gift.

Some people have a genuine knack of choosing gifts which count, but it is something that can be learned. The starting point is knowing and understanding the tastes, likes and interests of the recipient. The direct way is to ask "what would you really like me to buy you as a present?" It should ensure that you buy something that is wanted, but lacks somewhat in subtlety. Somewhat better is to ask for a few ideas or pointers. Actively and continuously listening and looking for ideas and signals long before the time comes to buy a present is the ideal way.

To buy a gift for the home requires consciously being aware of the taste, style and colour schemes which the person has already chosen. To give a gift of clothing is a very personal thing to do, especially for the opposite sex, and there is a risk that it will scarcely ever be worn or regarded as downright unsuitable. The chances of getting it right can be increased by carefully observing the taste, style, look and colours favoured by the recipient.

Some people have the knack of choosing exciting or unusual gifts, but again one has to be able to anticipate the response of the recipient. Exciting presents include activities such as a ride in the London Eye, a journey by steam train, a parachute jump, a session driving a racing car on a track. The list is endless, it requires thoughtfulness and a little imagination.

One test of a successful gift is that the recipient regards it as a treat or luxury they would never have bought for themselves. Another successful gift is the unusual item. People who seem repeatedly to manage to find unusual and desirable gifts make a point of continuously looking out for unusual items and know that the place to find unusual gifts is in individual shops rather than multiple stores.

Family and friends action plan

An executive summary is inadequate, you need to take positive action. The essence of investing time in your family and friends, is to improve your work life balance so that you do have the time to invest.

Failure to do so, may result in loneliness, regret and even despair. You cannot afford to adopt the attitude that becoming rich is everything, and you can attend to friends and family later, because by then it may be too late to repair the damage.

Use the following format, to create a personal action plan outlining specific things you will do.

Family and friends action plan

Your partner or spouse

_____

Your parents

_____

Your children

_____

Other relatives

_____

Friends and acquaintances

_____

Coping with separation and divorce

_____

Coping with bereavement and terminal illness

_____

Giving gifts that count

_____

ELIMINATE THE WORD 'RETIREMENT' FROM YOUR VOCABULARY AND REPLACE IT WITH 'REINVENTION'

10 Reinvention not retirement

MANY PEOPLE PURSUE WEALTH IN order to realize their dream of retiring early, for some this could be by the age of 40 or even sooner, because they imagine this will bring true happiness. The reality is very different in many cases. People suddenly realize that their self-esteem and sense of importance has been dealt a body blow and that much of their circle of friends and acquaintances was work related, as were their topics of conversation.

Suddenly being faced with nothing to do, may be a boring, lonely and difficult situation to handle. I remember meeting a 55 year old senior executive who was made redundant without any notice, but provided with full pension benefits. He told me that his entire world had collapsed and he had no reason to get out of bed or to get dressed and shaved. So much so that his health, happiness and his marriage really suffered, and he took a part-time job as a car park attendant to given him a purpose. It transformed his life, not least the brief social contact with his regular customers, and eventually got a full-time job collecting and delivering customers' cars for the service department of a local garage. Financially he did not need to work, but he really did need to work for his own well being. In real life, there are many versions of this story and it cannot be dismissed as an isolated situation.

The key to so called *'retirement'* at any age includes:

- dismiss any thought of retirement, think reinvention
- develop ideas and interests well ahead
- ease down to part-time work
- start a business or self-employment
- consider charity work
- build mental stimulus and social contact into your life
- learn for the hell of it
- keep abreast of technology
- exercise sensibly
- avoid a golden oldie ghetto lifestyle
- create and pursue a personal action plan.

Each of these will be considered separately.

Dismiss any thought of retirement, think reinvention

Many people who are presently working would probably define retirement as the time when you suddenly stop working. Retirement from full-time work happens for many people by the age of about 50, either by choice or redundancy. This means that they have worked for about 30 years, and now face a similar time 'retired' from full-time work.

Suddenly to stop work and do nothing is a recipe for disaster. Boredom, loneliness, apathy and a lack of any sense of purpose or direction are likely consequences. I suggest you eliminate the word 'retirement' from your vocabulary and replace it with 'reinvention'. You have to reinvent your lifestyle and interests for the next phase of your life. It requires planning ahead, application and a positive mental attitude, but potentially the reward is a long period of real happiness.

Develop ideas and interests well ahead

It is commonplace for so called successful people to find that their work and socializing with colleagues almost consumes their entire week. They may literally boast that they simply have neither the time nor need for other interests, because work is all consuming and satisfying. Does this sound like you? If so, recognize that to suddenly stop work will create a huge void in your life.

Some people mistakenly imagine that this will not be a problem, because they will tackle it when the time comes, but not before. Inertia and apathy, however, may mean that there will be a lengthy, boring and lonely void at the outset.

One thing is certain you should, and probably will, have time to pursue hobbies and interests. So think about interests which you have dropped through lack of time and new interests which you would like to explore. Use the internet to research the available opportunities so that you have developed ideas ready to put into action, or much better still, that you have already begun to pursue.

POTENTIALLY THE REWARD IS A LONG PERIOD OF REAL HAPPINESS

THE ART OF THE POSSIBLE IS A VITAL INGREDIENT OF SUCCESSFUL REINVENTION

Ease down to part-time work

Job sharing is increasingly commonplace. So why can't you suggest that you work part-time as a prelude to retirement, by handing over some of your work to other people. Although there may not be a precedent in your company, remember that the art of the possible is a vital ingredient of successful reinvention. So, ask!

If you own your own company, it is entirely possible to reallocate responsibilities so that you are able to work part-time for, say, two years or more before you sell the business. It does not mean that you need to lose effective control of the company and it will demonstrate management continuity without you to a potential acquirer.

If you are self-employed, you can choose to work part-time at any point and for as long as you wish. It simply requires the self-discipline to organize your diary accordingly and to accept a lower income.

The real benefit of switching to part-time work is that you have the opportunity to develop the interests and activities which will give you a satisfying life when you give up your present work completely.

Start a part-time business or self-employment

You could do this to earn money or to do something you enjoy, or both.

There are plenty of opportunities to make money from a hobby. An artist or wood carver could persuade local restaurants to display pieces of work on a sale or return basis. The enthusiastic gardener could offer to plant hanging baskets or to provide a garden design service.

LEARNING IS FUN. JUST DO IT FOR THE HELL AND ENJOYMENT OF IT

Even if you do not have a suitable hobby, read Chapter 6 again because the suggestions for self-employment or starting your own business are suitable to adopt part-time.

Another approach is to take a specialist course in order to create a part-time opportunity. Website design, photography, interior design, and cookery are just a few opportunities.

Consider charity work

Charity work is available in all shapes and sizes. It can range from occasionally helping out in a charity shop to a part-time, or even full-time, executive role. Specialist agencies exist either to provide local 'helping hand' opportunities or to place people in executive roles.

A part-time executive role needs serious commitment. You may be expected to commit to specific days to work each week, but of course the hours you work and the holidays you choose should give you adequate freedom. You will need to adapt your approach to work. The executive authority you enjoyed previously may not exist because your colleagues are volunteers. Also, you may find yourself 'reporting' to a full-time employee who is much less qualified and experienced than you, and much younger too.

Build mental stimulus and social contact in your life

Medical experts insist that mental stimulus and social contact are important ingredients for a healthy retirement.

You are surrounded by opportunities so there are no excuses available to you.

Here are a few ideas:

1 visit art galleries and, better still, join a conducted tour or lecture about the exhibition

2 go to see a serious play at the theatre

3 read the comment columns of serious newspapers and tackle the crossword

4 join a chess club or backgammon group

5 take up bridge, or re-ignite your previous interest in the game

6 join a book reading and discussion group or a play reading circle

7 attend lectures on local history or gardening.

Learn for the hell of it

Learning opportunities have never been more widely available. Local colleges offer a huge range of courses. Universities and some boarding schools organize residential summer schools to utilize their facilities during holiday periods. Art galleries run lecture courses. The internet has opened up every conceivable kind of distance learning opportunity.

Learning does not have to be to gain a qualification. Learning is fun. Just do it for the hell and enjoyment of it. If you feel you have a latent talent and never had the opportunity to explore it, now is the time. Popular craft courses include woodworking, cookery and art. Design opportunities include interior, textile and garden design.

Keep abreast of technology

To be in the mainstream of life, you need to keep abreast of technology because otherwise you will be confronted by ever increasing no go zones.

Governments are right to encourage everyone to be computer literate and to have internet access. Help is at hand. Computer courses aimed at the over 50's and those terrified by computers are widely available. They assume absolutely no previous knowledge whatsoever and are often arranged in modules so that you can progress from basic personal computer use to e-mailing and using the internet. If you are terrified not just of computers but the thought of a computer course, then consider finding a local trainer who will teach you the basics in your own home and help you choose a suitable first computer for beginners.

Exercise sensibly

It is never too late to start, even if you have been a lifelong couch potato, but the first step should be a check-up with your doctor. Sensible exercise means that you should start modestly. Loosen up and warm up at the start of a session, and never overdo exercise so that you are left with aches or pains.

You do not have to join a gym club or buy an exercise routine book, unless you want to, because you can build exercise into your daily routine by developing habits such as:

- walk to your local shops rather than driving
- collect your daily newspaper instead of having it delivered
- take every opportunity to walk up steps and don't use lifts or elevators
- arrange a weekly walk with a friend or join them in walking their dog (if you don't have one).

Medical opinion seems unanimous that a brisk walk is valuable exercise. A pedometer is a way of finding out how far you walk and setting personal goals to gradually increasing your walking. Pedometers measure distance covered and steps walked. The recommended activity level by medical experts is 10,000 steps a day.

Other opportunities to take exercise include:

- take up indoor or outdoor bowls
- join a rambling or walking group
- find a local par 3 golf course, which will probably offer a pay-as-you-play alternative to annual membership and play with a friend (it may prove a prelude to your taking up golf as a serious interest)
- many sports centres offer varied activity sessions for the over 50's

- join an exercise class
- play tennis, which can be enjoyed well into your 70's by most people
- swimming and cycling.

Avoid a golden oldie ghetto lifestyle

As some people become older, they retreat into a golden oldie ghetto lifestyle by joining clubs for old people and surrounding themselves with acquaintances who are old. It is to enter a world where people regularly reminisce about the old days being better.

Happiness requires you to deal with life as it is today and to embrace change.

An important way to do this is to mix with people of all ages and to understand their outlook and the pressures they face. So make sure that some of the activities you pursue are peopled by various age groups.

Personal action plan

It is all too easy to dismiss this chapter as being appropriate for other people, but not you, or to have good intentions and to do nothing about them. Everyone needs a personal action programme to maximize their happiness when, and ideally before, they give up full-time paid employment. So do use the following format to write down the action you are committed to take.

Personal action plan

Interests to develop or take up

_____

Part-time work or business activity

_____

Clubs to join

_____

Charity work opportunities

_____

Learning

_____

Technology

_____

Exercise

_____

11 Enjoy your wealth

WEALTH OFTEN PROVES TO BE a burden. Yes, really! Your reaction may be that when you become wealthy, you will be really happy and truly enjoy your money. Well, only time will tell.

Some people are so pre-occupied with passing on their wealth to children and grandchildren that they never enjoy it themselves. Some anxiously watch the price of their shares every day and worry when the stockmarket is falling. Money should be enjoyed and shared, as well as looked after to provide you with sufficient wealth to maintain your lifestyle throughout your life. The rest you can pass onto your children and grandchildren or give to charity.

Issues which need to be addressed include:

1. don't put all your eggs in one basket
2. don't attempt to walk on water
3. use an expert wealth manager or do-it-yourself
4. give your children and grandchildren the ultimate gift
5. tax effective giving

> 6 reward your own achievement
> 7 maintain a value for money attitude
> 8 be generous, but avoid hangers on
> 9 key point summary.

Each issue will be addressed separately.

Don't put all your eggs in one basket

The key to protecting your wealth is to spread your risk by deliberately allocating your investment across different asset types. It will not maximize the return on your investment, but will limit any losses you suffer.

Never forget the maxim that what goes up must come down. Investment advisers have demonstrated this by comparing the performance of a hypothetical portfolio of the ten best performing unit trusts or mutual funds in the previous year, with that of the ten worst performers, in a majority of years the worst performers have done better as they recovered. In the same way, never assume that because private equity investment has outperformed, say, commercial property for either one or several years it will continue to do so.

**MONEY SHOULD
BE ENJOYED
AND SHARED**

Don't attempt to walk on water

Entrepreneurs who have become wealthy by selling their company may be tempted to believe they can make a success of any business start-up or turn-round a failing company. They think their magic will work in every situation, and that their lack of any previous experience of the business sector is irrelevant.

The restaurant business seems particularly appealing, perhaps because the thought of playing host, meeting and greeting people, seems enjoyable and something of an ego trip brought to life. The truth is that the restaurant industry has consistently produced the highest level of business failures. To an outsider, the restaurant business appears deceptively simple, but it requires a shrewd assessment of the local market, an attractive décor and ambience, a carefully chosen menu and competitive pricing. Worst still, the key to success for many restaurants is a hands-on approach and constant attention to detail.

IT IS NOT ENOUGH TO BE SATISFIED THAT YOUR FUND HAS MADE A RETURN OF, SAY, 12% IN GERMANY DURING THE PAST YEAR IF THE BENCHMARK AVERAGE HAS RISEN BY OVER 30%

Use an expert wealth manager or do-it-yourself

Investments need regular monitoring, but a do-it-yourself approach is entirely possible and you may outperform an expert wealth manager.

In order to manage your investments effectively, you should be prepared to spend up to an hour a day reading business news pages and internet websites not only to monitor performance but to learn about anticipated trends and alternative investment opportunities. You must maintain detailed records to complete your annual tax return for dividend income and capital gains. Also, you need to have a dispassionate attitude towards your investments and be ready to sell poor performers and potential under-performers.

Performance measurement is a technique used by professional investors and fund managers, which you should adopt because it is not enough to be satisfied that you are making a profit overall.

Stock market investments should be measured by the appropriate bench market index. For example, in the UK there are separate indices for the 100 largest companies, the top 250, smaller companies and all shares. Shares, unit trusts or mutual funds of overseas companies should be compared with the index of the country concerned. It is not enough to be satisfied that your fund has made a return of, say, 12% in Germany during the past year if the benchmark average has risen by over 30%. Equally, by monitoring the index monthly you may be able to spot a falling trend, which looks as if it will continue, and to switch your investments elsewhere.

In soccer, in the FA Cup competition in the UK it is always possible that a small non-league team will beat a top team such as Manchester United, but it must be regarded as a one-off event because the odds are stacked against the smaller club. In the same way, the research resources and closeness to markets stacks the

THE ULTIMATE GIFT ONE CAN GIVE TO CHILDREN AND GRANDCHILDREN IS EDUCATION

odds in favour of expert wealth managers compared to the individual investor, but it does not guarantee superior performance.

One way to assess your own investments is to meet, say, three wealth management firms and ask them to critique your portfolio and to recommend for you:

- a preferred asset allocation
- investments they would sell
- investments they would make on your behalf.

The result could be that your investments are sound or you need to make some changes. Alternatively, they may persuade you that a management fee of about 1% annually, plus dealing costs, for a discretionary investment service is worthwhile because it will give you a superior return, access to some investment opportunities which you could not access yourself, such as a particular private equity or hedge fund, simplified administration and detailed tax information supplied to you. The choice is up to you.

Give your children and grandchildren the ultimate gift

I believe the ultimate gift one can give to children and grandchildren is education, because it is so enduring.

If you are satisfied with the existing state education available, then stick with it. If not, and there is an attractive school available in a different catchment area, consider moving house or helping your adult children to move for the benefit of your grandchildren.

If you feel it is preferable that your children or your grandchildren, provided the parents agree, should attend a fee paying school then be ready to pay for the privilege, making sure you can afford it throughout their school life.

On a much more modest scale, you may decide to pay for extra lessons, optional school trips, music or drama lessons or whatever. Spending a bit of money and, more importantly, giving your time to take children and grandchildren to the theatre, ballet and classical music concerts adds up to education in the wider sense.

In terms of university education, you may care to finance a child to attend an overseas university to widen their experience. Alternatively, you may wish to help finance a post-graduate qualification such as an MBA.

Tax effective giving

By the time you die there is every chance that your children will be over 50 and your grandchildren will have completed their education. To simply leave them a large sum of money in your will, even if sheltered from inheritance or death tax, is probably not the most generous or tax effective thing to do.

Find out what the current tax rules are for annual gifts, and giving out of surplus annual income, or on marriage, free of inheritance tax. In this way, you may be able to build a worthwhile capital sum for your children and grandchildren either to fund their university education or for a deposit to help them to buy their first home.

Furthermore, it should be possible to arrange that it is highly tax effective regarding interest income and capital gains, but do take expert advice at the outset.

You may wish to give to charity and most countries offer various tax effective opportunities, for giving small or large amounts. Income tax, capital gains tax and inheritance tax can be avoided, but it is essential to take expert advice before you make gifts to charities because the tax benefits may not apply retrospectively.

Reward your own achievement

This is not a recommendation to spend, spend and spend! It is a plea, however to reward your own achievement by giving yourself treats. This is not childish, but part of the feel good factor and self-esteem which are so important to becoming even wealthier and entirely consistent with enjoying your money sensibly along the way.

Neither is it a recipe to be flash or ostentatious. A good creed to adopt is quiet understatement, but you do need to look and act the part to feel entirely at home in the circles you wish to be a part of.

Maintain a value for money attitude

Recognize that freehold property will appreciate in real value over a decade, but cars and boats will depreciate rapidly.

An important financial priority should be to maintain your present lifestyle even if you suffer a major setback. So beware of living up to your income for the sake of it.

Think about saving and investing so that you can achieve financial independence for the rest of your life and freedom from the need to work to provide an income.

I have witnessed plenty of people with successful businesses who believed the good times could only get better, and spent accordingly. Then suddenly the business collapsed, in many cases caused by external factors.

These are the very people who would spend £200,000 on a whim to refurbish their kitchen, even though it was entirely acceptable in truth, and in any event could have been done at a fraction of the cost.

Be generous but avoid hangers-on

Successful boxers and football players are prime examples of what can happen when people suddenly have an income beyond their wildest dreams. They may claim to have kept their friends from before becoming rich, but actually only be paying for them to enjoy the highlife. So often, when the money runs out the so called friends drift away.

People much less well off than you will be thrilled to enjoy an indulgent treat occasionally, but friendship is a two-way street. They will want to do things with you which allows them to pay their way and occasionally treat you.

A surfeit of vintage champagne, the finest wines, high stake gambling, drugs and mindless extravagance is a pale substitute for genuine happiness.

Key point summary

1 spread your investment to minimize risk

2 don't imagine you are an infallible winner, time will prove you wrong

3 consider appointing a wealth manager, particularly if you worry about your wealth

4 recognize that education is the ultimate gift you can give your children and grandchildren

5 take advantage of tax effective gifts, including charitable donations

6 reward your achievement by treating yourself

7 maintain a value for money outlook

8 be generous, but be wary of hangers-on.

Other titles from Thorogood

EXIT RIGHT

Achieving a golden goodbye by realizing the maximum value for your business

Barrie Pearson
£16.99 paperback, £35.00 hardback
Published September 2004

This book offers comprehensive, streetwise and practical 'how to' help for every step involved in selling or floating your business. Various exit routes are considered, as he explains all the steps required to maximize the profit from your sale: deciding on the route and timing, how to choose advisers, grooming your business for disposal, valuing the business, finding prospective purchasers, negotiating the sale, steering safely to completion and how to eliminate losses before selling. This book is a goldmine of expert advice, written by a highly skilled professional who later employed his own advice to achieve spectacular success.

THE BOOK OF ME

Life coach yourself to success

"Never mind e-commerce – what about Me-commerce?"

Barrie Pearson and Neil Thomas
£14.99 paperback, £24.99 hardback
Published January 2003

Me-commerce is the mechanism by which you can develop and exploit your assets, skills and character to achieve both personal and financial success and balance in your life.

"We make plans for *other people*. We make profits for *them*. We think strategically at work but not at home" But where does this leave *you*? Here is a manual to help you realize your full potential, by putting yourself first for a change.

DEVELOPING AND MANAGING TALENT
How to match talent to the role and convert it to a strength

Sultan Kermally
£12.99 paperback, £24.99 hardback
Published May 2004

Effective talent management is crucial to business development and profitability. Talent management is no soft option; on the contrary, it is critical to long-term survival.

This book offers strategies and practical guidance for finding, developing and above all keeping talented individuals. After explaining what developing talent actually means to the organization, he explores the e-dimension and the global dimension. He summarizes what the 'gurus' have to say on the development of leadership talent. Included are valuable case studies drawn from Hilton, Volkswagen, Unilever, Microsoft and others.

GURUS ON BUSINESS STRATEGY
Tony Grundy
£14.99 paperback, £24.99 hardback
Published May 2003

This book is a one-stop guide to the world's most important writers on business strategy. It expertly summarises all the key strategic concepts and describes the work and contribution of each of the leading thinkers in the field.

It goes further: it analyses the pro's and con's of many of the key theories in practice and offers two enlightening case-studies. The third section of the book provides a series of detailed checklists to aid you in the development of your own strategies for different aspects of the business.

More than just a summary of the key concepts, this book offers valuable insights into their application in practice.

SUCCESSFUL BUSINESS PLANNING
Norton Paley
£14.99 paperback, £29.99 hardback
Published June 2004

"Growth firms with a written business plan have increased their revenues 69 per cent faster over the past five years than those without a written plan."
FROM A SURVEY BY PRICEWATERHOUSECOOPERS

We know the value of planning – in theory. But either we fail to spend the time required to go through the thinking process properly, or we fail to use the plan effectively. Paley uses examples from real companies to turn theory into practice.

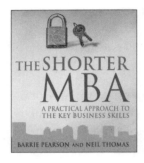

THE SHORTER MBA

A practical approach to the key business skills

Barrie Pearson and Neil Thomas

£35.00 Hardback • Published July 2004

A succinct distillation of the skills that you need to be successful in business. Most people can't afford to give up two years to study for an MBA. This pithy, practical book presents all the essential theory, practice and techniques taught to MBA students – ideal for the busy practising executive. It is divided into three parts:

- Personal development
- Management skills
- Business development

Thorogood also has an extensive range of reports and special briefings which are written specifically for professionals wanting expert information.

For a full listing of all Thorogood publications, or to order any title, please call Thorogood Customer Services on 020 7749 4748 or fax on 020 7729 6110. Alternatively view our website at: **www.thorogood.ws**.

BUSINESS SEMINARS

Focused on developing your potential

Falconbury, the sister company to Thorogood publishing, brings together the leading experts from all areas of management and strategic development to provide you with a comprehensive portfolio of action-centred training and learning.

We understand everything managers and leaders need to be, know and do to succeed in today's commercial environment. Each product addresses a different technical or personal development need that will encourage growth and increase your potential for success.

- Practical public training programmes
- Tailored in-company training
- Coaching
- Mentoring
- Topical business seminars
- Trainer bureau/bank
- Adair Leadership Foundation

The most valuable resource in any organization is its people; it is essential that you invest in the development of your management and leadership skills to ensure your team fulfil their potential. Investment into both personal and professional development has been proven to provide an outstanding ROI through increased productivity in both you and your team. Ultimately leading to a dramatic impact on the bottom line.

With this in mind Falconbury have developed a comprehensive port-folio of training programmes to enable managers of all levels to develop their skills in leadership, communications, finance, people manage-ment, change management and all areas vital to achieving success in today's commercial environment.

What Falconbury can offer you?

- Practical applied methodology with a proven results
- Extensive bank of experienced trainers
- Limited attendees to ensure one-to-one guidance
- Up to the minute thinking on management and leadership techniques
- Interactive training
- Balanced mix of theoretical and practical learning
- Learner-centred training
- Excellent cost/quality ratio

Falconbury In-Company Training

Falconbury are aware that a public programme may not be the solution to leadership and management issues arising in your firm. Involving only attendees from your organization and tailoring the programme to focus on the current challenges you face individually and as a business may be more appropriate. With this in mind we have brought together our most motivated and forward thinking trainers to deliver tailored in-company programmes developed specifically around the needs within your organization.

All our trainers have a practical commercial background and highly refined people skills. During the course of the programme they act as facilitator, trainer and mentor, adapting their style to ensure that each individual benefits equally from their knowledge to develop new skills.

Falconbury works with each organization to develop a programme of training that fits your needs.

Mentoring and coaching

Developing and achieving your personal objectives in the workplace is becoming increasingly difficult in today's constantly changing environment. Additionally, as a manager or leader, you are responsible for guiding colleagues towards the realization of their goals. Sometimes it is easy to lose focus on your short and long-term aims.

Falconbury's one-to-one coaching draws out individual potential by raising self-awareness and understanding, facilitating the learning and performance development that creates excellent managers and leaders. It builds renewed self-confidence and a strong sense of 'can-do' competence, contributing significant benefit to the organization. Enabling you to focus your energy on developing your potential and that of your colleagues.

Mentoring involves formulating winning strategies, setting goals, monitoring achievements and motivating the whole team whilst achieving a much improved work life balance.

Falconbury – Business Legal Seminars

Falconbury Business Legal Seminars specialises in the provision of high quality training for legal professionals from both in-house and private practice internationally.

The focus of these events is to provide comprehensive and practical training on current international legal thinking and practice in a clear and informative format.

Event subjects include, drafting commercial agreements, employment law, competition law, intellectual property, managing an in-house legal department and international acquisitions.

For more information on all our services please contact Falconbury on +44 (0)20 7729 6677 or visit the website at: www.falconbury.co.uk.